The Continuing Heartcry for China

Ross Paterson

Sovereign World

Sovereign World Ltd
PO Box 777
Tonbridge
Kent TN11 0ZS
England

ISBN: 1-85240-268-7

This Sovereign World book is distributed in North America by Renew
Books, a ministry of Gospel Light, Ventura, California, USA. For a free
catalog of resources from Renew Books/Gospel Light, please contact your
Christian supplier or call 1-800-4-GOSPEL.

Typeset by CRB Associates, Reepham, Norfolk.
Printed in England by Clays Ltd, St Ives plc.

Contents

103914

Foreword

*For Christ's love compels us, because we are convinced that
one died for all, and therefore all died. And he died for all,
that those who live should no longer live for themselves but
for him who died for them and was raised again...*

(2 Corinthians 5:14,15 NIV)

Ross Paterson has written a compelling book about a compelling love. It speaks in simple and moving terms about
Christ's love for the great nation of China; it speaks of the
extraordinary new life evidenced there through His death; it
speaks of what may yet come about there through His life.

I knew Ross by reputation some years before I was privileged to know him as a friend and recognised in him the
qualities of a man of God. He had made brave choices which
were against the tide of the times and it was clear that these
came from an intimate relationship with Jesus and obedience
to His voice. Even this book is a result of the choices he
speaks of in the last chapter. I believe that through the
information and passion contained within, many will hear
the voice that begged him to be its mouthpiece.

I would advise it as required reading for those concerned in
any way with the Far East. I would also recommend it to all
who claim to be followers of Jesus Christ, with the prayer
that it be used as a tool in the universal commission.

Jackie Pullinger
Hong Kong

Dedication

To Christine, my *airen*,

and

Deborah, Hannah, Sharon, Joanna and Esther,
our five 'golden flowers'.

Author's Preface and Introduction to Second Edition

This book sets out to report the very real needs of the Chinese churches and to challenge Christians worldwide to face up to those needs. In the ten years since it was first published, much has happened in China. This second edition is a completely new one, with much fresh material and significant additions that reflect the changes in China and in the ministry to China in which I am engaged. The heartcry, however, remains the same. My plea is that Christians should not forget the needs of the Chinese people. I have been in close touch with developments in the Chinese Church for many years now, and with those working both inside and outside of China. Many of those believers want the world to know the truth about their situation. This book is written for your urgent attention on their behalf. It is a practical one. It contains practical suggestions for those who want to respond in specific ways to this great and fascinating people and the Church amongst them.

There are many who have helped with the task of preparing this book. First and foremost, my wife Christine. She was closeted with me in Louisville, Kentucky, and in Chiangmai, Thailand, doing little else day and night but writing. She takes much credit for the work. Indeed, the book is dedicated to her and to my five daughters. They are precious gifts from the Lord and I thank Him for them. They know more than any around me the cost of serving China.

Christine Hobson did an initial rewrite and then edited every chapter as it was written and rewritten. She did an enormous amount of work in her usual humble and effective way. She has been a great gift to me and to the ministry. I doubt the book would have happened without her.

Craig Dahlberg also worked with us, combining his great gifts – in literature, computers and humour (sorry, Craig, humor). All three of those gifts, not the least the last one, were a great blessing to us in some long days and short nights. Jackie, thanks!

Thanks are due too to Lita for her thorough work in helping us prepare the chapter on China's minorities in particular. Ian, James and David also gave much key material – apart from being fantastic people.

And that is not to exclude many others in our China team – scattered across two ministries, many lands, and much gifting. If I mention one, then I have to mention all. Brothers and sisters, you are special. Consider yourself mentioned – please. Thank you that what is shared in this book is not theory, but reality, because you under God have made it so by your faith and your courage and obedience.

There are so many others from other ministries, China and beyond, who have influenced and helped. Again, if I mention one, how do I not mention the others? Please then let me leave you to have your reward with the Master!

Then there are my parents. They are very wonderful people, and I am deeply grateful to them for their patience and support. Few sons could have been so blessed in their parents as I have been! It has not been easy for you to put up with a son with such a calling; I appreciate you so much.

Christine's father went to be with the Lord between the two editions of this book. Her parents were for many years missionaries in Africa, and now her Mum is back there – in her eighties. What a model!

We also moved to Singapore between the two editions. Alec and Gillian, we could not and would not have managed that without you. How can we thank you enough? Danny and Mona, John L., David C., Philip and Buang Kher, Corinne... There are so many more.

God has given us great colleagues in the China ministry in Singapore, and we are grateful to every one of you. Singapore has a special place in ministry to China, and it is my fervent prayer that she would fully become an 'Antioch'.

Brenda, thanks for the loan of your apartment in Louisville, and to you, Bill and Barbara, for arranging that; Kendall and Gina, thanks for all your kindness that mixed fun into the long hours in Chiangmai. You did a good job there, Alvin!

Finally, there are my brothers and sisters in China. Thank you for walking with the Lord Jesus; thank you for living – and dying – for Him.

Section A

Chapter 1

The Birth of This Book

A group of Western Christians who had been serving the Lord on a short-term mission team in China were travelling back to Hong Kong by train. As they journeyed across China's huge and historic land, they fell into conversation with their fellow passengers. The topic of the conversation turned to the claims of the Lord Jesus Christ on the lives of every man and woman, and of His wonderful provision of life for us through His death on the cross and subsequent resurrection.

As the train wound its way slowly across China, the conversation was unhurried, cumbered as it was with the need for translation. One young man sat there, listening but not contributing. It was not possible to know what was on his mind, or if he were hostile to such a conversation taking place in public in Communist China. Suddenly after about two hours he spoke, signifying that he wanted to ask a question. His question was as direct as it was delayed: 'If there really is such good news as this, the good news of the love of God in Jesus,' he asked, 'why have I never heard of this before? Why has no one told us?'

Why indeed? Why had he not heard – and more than one billion people like him in China?

This question is no easier to answer now than it was more than a century ago, when the great missionary pioneer to China, James Hudson Taylor, faced the same challenge. Taylor, founder of the China Inland Mission, was burdened by the millions of Chinese passing into a Christless eternity. At the beginning of his work he led a young man to Christ, Brother Ni. As their relationship developed and Ni became involved in the work of the Lord, there came a day when he

felt free enough to ask Hudson Taylor a question: 'How long
have your people in Europe known about Jesus and His way
of salvation?' Taylor answered that the gospel had been
available to a greater or lesser extent in Europe for hundreds
of years. 'If that is so,' replied Brother Ni, 'why did my father
in China have to search for the truth for twenty years – and
die without ever finding it?'

Why indeed? Why had he not heard?

Hudson Taylor's response is now history. Shortly after that,
while in England on leave from his work in China, he was
attending a church service on the south coast, in a town
called Brighton. The question that Ni had put to him and the
burden for China's lost millions lay heavily on him. But this
was apparently not the case for many of the other believers
who worshipped God in that church on that significant
Sunday morning. They seemed largely unconcerned for the
world's lost. Taylor walked out of the meeting – not out of
rebellion or anger, but because of his burden for China. He
walked on Brighton beach, not for the benefit of the
sunshine (remember he was in England!) but lost in deep
prayer with the Lord. He cried out to God to provide him
with twenty-four willing and able workers to go with him to
China. His response was a specific one – and so was the
Lord's. Indeed the small group of men and women that
the Lord raised up in answer to prayer became the nucleus
of the China Inland Mission, one of the greatest missionary
organisations there has ever been. The CIM was to reach deep
into many parts of China with the good news of Christ.

Around that time Taylor wrote:

> My soul yearns, oh how intensely, for the evangelisation
> of the 180 millions [now 1250 millions] of these unoc-
> cupied provinces. Oh, that I had a hundred lives to give
> or spend for their good! One third of the human family
> is in China, needing the Gospel. Twelve millions [now
> many more] there are passing beyond the reach of that
> Gospel every year. If you want hard work and little
> appreciation; if you value God's approval more than
> you fear men's disapprobation; if you are prepared to
> take joyfully the spoiling of your goods, and seal your

testimony, if need be, with your blood; if you can pity and love the Chinese, you may count on a harvest of souls now and a crown of glory hereafter 'that fadeth not away', and on the Master's 'Well done'.[1]

It is necessary at this point, as I begin the second and revised version of this book, to issue both a definition and a challenge – to draw, if you like, a line in the sand. In one way or another, China demands that we respond, as Hudson Taylor did those many years ago. That will mean breaking the norm to obey the Lord.

Paul states in 1 Corinthians 8:1 that, *'Knowledge puffs up, but love edifies.'* Paul was not hostile to knowledge. Indeed in Romans 10:2 he made it clear that the absence of knowledge, particularly in the context of misdirected zeal, could be dangerous and even eternally fatal. Paul's own preconversion life was one in which the absence of knowledge led him into devastating and costly error.

No, Paul was talking about knowledge that accumulates and even boasts of information, but does not follow through to defined action. Love, however, demands that we not only inform ourselves about the world and analyse its needs, but that we change our attitudes and actions – even the course of our lives – in response to what we know.

The account of Paul's own conversion in Acts 9 is a classic illustration of this. He obtained from Jesus by revelation the answer to three questions, each of which can be summed up by one word.

The first word is *'Who'*. In Acts 9:5 Paul, confronted by the blinding revelation of Jesus on the road to Damascus, asked a very simple but very defining question. He said, *'Who are You, Lord?'* Then the Lord said, *'I am Jesus, whom you are persecuting. It is hard for you to kick against the goads.'*

The answer to the 'Who' was of course Jesus Christ. From that moment Paul received, not just knowledge about Jesus, but Jesus Himself. The encounter totally and radically changed him. Up to that point he had persecuted even to death any who believed in Jesus. Now, as a result of that personal encounter with Jesus, he was prepared to put himself in the firing line. His was a totally transforming personal encounter with the Saviour.

I trust your encounter with Jesus has been equally transforming. It certainly is for those who follow Him in China today.

Many of us might like to stop there. But we have to read on. Jesus and Paul on that Damascus road dealt with a second word – *'what'*. Acts 9:6 tells us that Paul, even though he was 'trembling and astonished', immediately asked a second question: *'Lord, **what** do You want me to do?'* The Lord responded to him, *'Arise and go into the city, and you will be told **what** you must do.'*

The clarity of that question and reply relates to the way that Paul addressed Jesus from the start – he called Him 'Lord'. Paul came from a very different, and much more biblical, place than many of us do today. It never occurred to Paul to doubt that the Lord God had the right to his obedience. He was called to serve the Lord His God with all his heart and soul and mind and strength – with everything that he had. The only issue that needing settling was **who** Jesus was. If He truly was the Son of the living God, it followed, logically and necessarily, that He had the right to tell Paul what to do with the rest of his life. If Jesus were Lord, then Paul needed from the moment of his conversion to know what he should do to serve Him for the rest of his life on earth.

That is what this book is all about. It is not only intended to be material that helps us to be informed. It is about the 'what' in our lives. It is about recognising that God is at work in our world, as exemplified by China, and that the call Jesus gave to Paul is most immediately relevant to us today. Ananias was told to put aside his fears and to set Paul free from his blindness and powerlessness. He was to pray that Paul might receive his sight and be filled with the Holy Spirit. That was specifically because he (Paul) was *'a chosen vessel of Mine to bear My Name before Gentiles'* (v. 15). Paul was to take the gospel to the unreached. One obvious application for us today is the nation of China. Multitudes of them are still unreached with the gospel.

I am aware that not all are called to China, that the 'what' for many will be something quite different. Yet our spirituality and deep experiences of God seem often to stop with the 'Who' of our personal encounter and fail to press on to the 'what' which embraces the needs of a dying world. One of the greatest scandals in the Church today is the absence of teaching and obedience to the Great Commission (Matthew 28:18–20; Acts 1:8). When God calls us, there is a 'what' in His plan for each one of us, for which we will give account if we are not obedient and faithful in fulfilling it. It may not be China; it may be some other part of the harvest field. But if the Holy Spirit is powerfully at work anywhere, as He is in China, does that not indicate that His Church should also be investing there, engaging in that work with all she has and is? If we are failing to do so wholeheartedly, perhaps it is because we are more interested in enjoying the 'Who' than in recognising the right of the Lord to speak forth His 'what' into our lives.

A third word that was central to that Damascus encounter between Paul and Jesus is the word *'how'* (or more accurately 'how much'). In Acts 9:16 Jesus proclaimed these words to Ananias about Paul: *'I will show him **how much** he must suffer for my name'* (NIV). The 'how' is a word denoting quantity, which Jesus relates to the issue of suffering – not a favourite concept for any of us, but an important one to grapple with none the less! The 'how' for Paul was not a word about the quantity of prosperity he would achieve by his new decision. It was a word of how much it would *cost* him so that others, the Gentiles, should prosper eternally in the presence of Jesus. It costs us to follow Jesus. This way of life is not easy at times.

Selwyn Hughes, writing recently on the subject of the Fatherhood of God, referred to 1 Peter 4:12:

> *Dear friends, do not be surprised at the painful trial you are suffering, as though something strange were happening to you!*

Hughes commented:

> What else can we learn from Scripture about our heavenly Father? This: He will not keep us from trouble but He will keep us in it. Why am I making this point? Because some suffer from misperceptions of their

heavenly Father ... One man told me recently while I was in the Far East that he had been brought up in a church where the evangelistic thrust was based on this theme: become a Christian and you will never have any troubles again. He became a Christian on that basis and found that whatever troubles he had before were as nothing compared to those he experienced following his conversion. He lost his job, his family turned their backs on him, and his girlfriend jilted him at the altar – all because he would not renounce his belief in Christ. When Christian leaders hold out the hope that becoming a Christian means freedom from trouble, they push converts towards disillusionment. The theology appears attractive and may help draw people towards Christianity, but it is not true. In 1 Peter 4:12 our Lord made it clear that we should expect trouble in this world. Followers of Christ suffer as much as others, sometimes more so. Those who believe that being a Christian will insulate them from adversity may well find their faith collapsing when they are under stress. What Scripture teaches is this: God will not save us from hardship, but He will save us in it.

In the prayer at the end of those comments, Selwyn Hughes wrote:

Father, help me understand that the world is a battleground, not a playground.[2]

Is it because we do not want to face the 'how' of the cost that we will not face the 'what' of the Great Commission, for China and for the nations? Is it possible that we are looking for a playground and not a battleground?

What is then the purpose of this book? It is my hope that, in the context of China, God might help each one of us to find more of the 'Who', and more of the 'what' (perhaps, for some, for the first time) and the 'how' of His calling.

I wish that I could introduce you to many of my colleagues in the ministry to China, to show you how the 'what' of God's calling has impacted and changed their lives.

There is the pastor from a Western country, who, when I first challenged him to be involved in China, politely declined. He said he was called to pastor local churches. But he is a man who hears God, and so he was willing to change his mind. Consequently he is now fully engaged with China. Men and women have found Jesus in China because he gave second thoughts to that 'what'. A man of exceptional obedience to the Spirit of God, he did not find the full expression of that obedience, nor of the manifestations of the Spirit of God in His life, until He became obedient to the 'what' of China.

Then there is a headmaster of a state school, who offered us a few months of free time to serve the Church in China, and who subsequently allowed God to speak to him about longer involvement. His dedication, efficiency and faith have resulted in literally hundreds of thousands of books being placed in the hands of Chinese believers, as he obeys the call of the Lord in a costly way.

Or the pastor from the UK, who a number of years ago went on a missions trip to China. He flew out of Hong Kong at the end of the China trip with a firm dedication that he would never, ever, go back to China again – he had not enjoyed himself! But the Lord spoke to him at 31,000 feet, and by the time he landed in the UK, he was planning the next trip! He has now led teams that have helped hundreds of people to serve the Lord in China.

There is also a sister who was brought up in a mix of Asian and Western values. Out of that she heard the Lord call her to China. She has faced reversal and even heartbreak, but she has pressed through in response to her calling. She remains one of the most trustworthy and effective team members that we have in the ministry, carving out a whole new area of outreach in the ministry to China.

There are many more. Indeed, even as I write I fear that by mentioning one or two I could offend others of my beloved colleagues by leaving them out! Each one has paid a price, and each one has responded not just in knowledge but in love, bringing life and change and blessing to multitudes of Chinese people, whether those who do not yet know Jesus, or believers in the churches, or children in orphanages. These people have brought life and direction also into the lives of many in their home countries, by helping them to engage with China, and thus helping them to pray for China, to give for China and to go to China.

May God help each of us, as we read these pages, to encounter (of course) the 'Who' of the Damascus road in our own experience, but to get beyond just the blessing of knowing Him as Saviour until we engage fully with the 'what' of His call on our lives. May He help us to get up from the floor (Paul was face-down on the road when the con-versation took place) and not stop going until we finish the race. Paul could have 'marketed' his Damascus road encoun-ter. It was a huge spiritual experience that was worth many meetings on the Christian circuit! But he was not that kind of a man. Though he knew it would cost him everything, he pressed beyond the 'Who' to the 'what'. May God do the same in our lives today.

The first part of this book is intended to help you to obey the 'what'. These chapters will suggest to you some practical ways in which you can respond to the Lord. The second part of the book deals with the more informational topics, the history and background of China and its Church. I hope you will read both. But it would be acceptable for you only to read the first half – as long as you act in at least some of the ways that Paul did in response to his divine encounter.

That is the nature of the heartcry in this book. My longing is that we should get beyond church activities and mission theory, beyond personal problems and needs, beyond ecclesi-astical politics and theoretical analysis. And that we should do, as the Lord leads, what Hudson Taylor did – take specific and defined steps to care for China and her Church.

It is ten years since I wrote the first edition of this book. Much has changed, both within China and in our ministry to China over the past ten years. This fully revised and increased edition reflects the situation ten years on and into a new millennium. The Lord has multiplied His work in China – with more workers, more literature, more radio, more prayer. But the heartcry is just the same: Lord, let the believers outside of China see that this is Your day of favour for that great land, and that we need to involve ourselves in Your purposes for her.

It has been my privilege to serve the Church in China for over thirty years now. The challenge of Hudson Taylor and of Brother Ni and of a multitude of others like the man on the train remains as much a divine imperative to me now as when I began. The voices are so many and so compelling – if we will hear them.

Even as I write these words, astonishing reports continue to come in of God's sovereign activity in China. A respected colleague, who has been involved for a number of years in the production of Christian literature for China, writes:

> Both the growth and the perseverance of the Chinese house church are phenomenal. Several months ago, believers I was with spoke of church growth by generations. One evangelist said that in some areas they experience seven to eight generations of new believers each year. That means that, on average, every new believer will lead another person to Christ within six or seven weeks of becoming a Christian themselves. Another young pastor said that, if we followed him for two weeks, we could see three or four generations of new Christians. This tremendous growth of the church is wonderful, but causes a great need for Bibles and teaching materials.

Elsewhere, from central China a believer wrote:

> Our church suffered persecution and was scattered in the spring of 1996. But since the autumn of last year, the believers have built up the church again. The cell group of a dozen people led by me has been continuing to evangelise, so now we have 170–180 people.

A church leader from the area bordering Mongolia told how, in the past five years or so, his church had grown from a handful to four to five hundred people. A believer from Shanxi province wrote:

> Christianity has expanded fast here in recent years. More and more house churches have been set up with evangelistic meetings . . . More and more people have been saved.

A revival of astonishing proportions is taking place behind the Bamboo Curtain. The Holy Spirit is moving sovereignly across the land of China, sweeping people into the Kingdom of God in their thousands, even millions.

Does the evidence of this revival negate the young man's challenge to our team on the train, the man who wondered why he had never heard the good news? Does it encourage us to ignore China on the grounds that there is no place nor need for our involvement? It should not, even though sometimes it does seem to have that effect. Such mistaken thinking misses three key elements of the China equation.

First, even if there are today as many as one hundred million believers in China, there would still be almost a billion who have not yet heard the gospel. The numbers being saved are truly amazing. But the population is so huge[3] that large areas of the country remain almost unreached, as do many of the minority people groups.

Second, because of this amazing growth of the Church, a large proportion of believers are without Bibles, teaching materials or training of any consistent nature. They are experiencing a 'famine' that will never capture the world's headlines, but which is just as real to them as the desperate physical plight of so many in drought-stricken lands. They are starving spiritually because of the lack of the Word of God. They are desperate to be able to read a Bible and to hear it expounded.

One itinerant evangelist went with some fellow believers to the countryside to evangelise. As soon as it became known in the area that he had arrived, people came from miles around, some walking day and night, so that they could attend an evening meeting that was scheduled to last a couple of hours. When the preacher had finished what he had to say, they begged him to continue so that they could hear more of God's Word. They were not prepared to let him eat or sleep, or to do so themselves, in order to take full advantage of the opportunity to digest 'spiritual food'.

Third, we do not know how long the 'window of opportunity' to serve and help in China may last. In 1968, I had the opportunity to take Christian literature into another Communist land, Czechoslovakia. At that time, the Church was enjoying considerable freedom under the liberal policies of Alexander Dubcek, policies which ushered in the brief period known as the 'Dubcek Spring'. We were allowed to hold a young people's camp in the mountains that summer, teaching the Word of God to the young people who came. It was a special and unusual time with the young Christians of that country. The atmosphere was good and relatively easygoing, and we took advantage of it. I can remember a Czech pastor saying to me, as he relished these opportunities for sharing the gospel and for building up the believers, that it had been twenty years since he had seen or known such a time of freedom and opportunity for the Church in Czechoslovakia.

One fateful day, however, everything changed. The door suddenly slammed shut again, just as quickly as it had opened. The Russian tanks rolled aggressively over Czechoslovakia's borders, and Dubcek's administration came to an abrupt end. The borders were tightened up, and a very hard season again came for the Church in that land. For years to come, nothing was as it had been during those few short months of freedom. So quickly can a situation change in a nation.

China has experienced a thawing in its relations with other countries, and a considerable relaxing in the tight grip that prevailed over people in the country, and especially in the Church, up to 1976. There is a partially open door through which tourists can go to visit this great land, and which professionals can use if they wish to work in China and to serve its people in their chosen field. It is also a door which Christians can utilise in various other ways, some of which will be detailed in later chapters of this book. Just how long the door will remain ajar is impossible to say.

The lesson of Czechoslovakia in 1968 must not be forgotten. That lesson is simple: if the door to such a land is even partly open, then the Church of Jesus Christ outside must help those inside in any way they request, and they must help them swiftly. If they express needs to us, then we must respond to those needs. We should not wait, nor put it on the agenda for some time in the future. The reason for that is simple – we do not know if there will be a future like the present time. Policies in China have been known to swing violently from one extreme to another on many occasions. We need to act now, and if the door should close later, we will have all the time we want for meditative inaction on the subject!

Many people see the present open door policy of China as God's answer to prayer. Having prayed it open, dare we ignore it when we have the resources to meet many of the needs of our brethren? Having seen God turn the events of China's history, will we not seek Him to do it again, and to open the door wider than it has yet been? I pray that it will be so.

John Angell James was a man burdened for China more than a hundred years ago. He saw the opportunity and the challenge for Christians outside of China to take spiritual advantage of the open door and to help China's Church. He had a long-standing friendship with Robert Morrison, one of the great early missionary pioneers to China. James had already organised an appeal to send a million New Testaments to China through the British and Foreign Bible Society. The appeal was so successful that twice that number – two million New Testaments – were sent to China. So James was not given to theory in the matter of serving China's Church.

In 1858, the year before he died, James penned these words:

> The conversion of China is, one way or another, the business of every Christian upon earth – and every Christian upon earth can do something for it and ought to do what he can. The man who says, 'What have I to do with this matter?' is either ignorant, indolent or covetous, and is altogether heartless towards the cause of Christ. He that says, 'What concern have I in China's conversion?', just asks the question, 'What fellowship have I with

Christ?' We are all too apt to think of what the Church can do and ought to do, and not what we individually can do and ought to do, and either through modesty, timidity or avarice, we lose ourselves and our individual obligations in the crowd. Do you then ask whose business the conversion of China is? I answer, 'Yours, whosoever you are who may read this page. Yours,' I say, 'as truly as that of any other man on the face of the earth.' Here it is, I offer it to you, and in the Name of Christ bid you take it. Take it into your hand, your heart, your purse, your closet – you dare not refuse it!

Perhaps we find that kind of language and challenge a trifle strong. Should it today not be even stronger, given the massive population growth in China and the corresponding growth in spiritual need? Dare we say the words are any less relevant today? For that voice now has its modern equivalents within China that give the same message in other forms.

May God have mercy on us. It is my prayer that He might use the second edition of this book even more powerfully than He used the first. There have been those that God in His mercy touched through the first edition and helped to find their place in service for the Church in China. May God raise up a multitude of servants of the cross of Christ who, in Hudson Taylor's words '. . . can pity and love the Chinese, (and) count on a harvest of souls now and a crown of glory hereafter "that fadeth not away", and on the Master's "Well done."'

Notes

1. Hudson Taylor's 'An appeal for prayer on behalf of more than 150 millions of Chinese', dated 1875.
2. Selwyn Hughes, *The Fatherhood of God* (CWR).
3. The current population of China is said to be 1.2 billion. In order to gain an inkling how many people that figure represents, consider one staggering statistic: there are more people alive in Mainland China today than there have been minutes since the time of Christ!

Chapter 2

Voicing the Silent Cry

Please be a reporter for us. We have no means by which our voice can be heard by others, inside or outside of China. Simply say to our brothers and sisters outside of China, 'Some people tell one story, and their voice is heard. But others are telling a different story, and their voice is not being heard.'

It was the early 1980s in Shanghai, the most populous of China's many large cities. China at that time was going through one of its frequent changes – or lurches – politically and socially. Indeed at that very time, the Gang of Four,[1] who had so brutalised the nation during the period of the Cultural Revolution in China, were on trial for their crimes against the nation and the people of China. A different leadership under Deng Xiaoping[2] was in charge, with new and more open policies, at least in the economic sphere. The curtain that separated China from the rest of the world had been pulled slightly aside, so that we could see a little of them and they of us. The Chinese were beginning to breathe again, though very carefully. There had been so much suffering and death during that dark period from 1966 to 1976, and the pain and suspicion were still very real.

I considered the couple before me in that simple room. Mr and Mrs Chen, Renguang and Enhui (not their real names), were Christian leaders, helping to lead and feed spiritually many believers in and around the city. They were of an age to have walked through the early days of Marxism in China in the 1950s, followed by the yet more difficult days of the

Cultural Revolution in the late 1960s and early 1970s. What they said did not come out of an immature or hotheaded enthusiasm; their words were born out of many years of suffering for the Lord Jesus Christ and for His gospel. They loved the Lord Jesus deeply, and their zeal for Him was as real as ever.

I had been nervous and excited as I approached the address that I had been given, for it was one of the first visits of that kind that I had made in China. But as I sat with them, I was welcomed because of the name of a mutual friend, which I had already mentioned to them. I was at ease with them and they with me.

I was astonished and even amused at the response they made to the Christian literature and tapes that I had handed over to them. If only my Christian friends outside China could see what I was seeing! Here were these two saints, well on in years, behaving like my children used to do when they were younger on being given birthday presents. Renguang and Enhui were excited and thrilled as they took out the books and tapes which would mean spiritual food for them to share with others.

Oriental people often tend to be polite and diffident before coming to the main point of what they want to say. But the Chens clearly trusted me and wanted no delays. They came straight to the point. They must have sat down before I arrived and prepared a 'shopping list' of topics for which they needed teaching material. Now I scribbled hasty notes in my little notebook, grateful that they spoke clear Mandarin Chinese without a local Shanghai accent. How wonderful it would be if many believers from abroad could see what I was seeing – such hunger for the Word of God, the way in which books and tapes were snapped up, and more asked for, almost before they were out of my bag.

I often reflect, as I consider people like the Chens, on the steps that brought me to their simple room that night. While I was a student at Cambridge University in the 1960s, Jesus in His mercy confronted me with the issue of His Lordship in my life. He was already my Saviour. That had been settled at the age of fourteen. But He wanted more. He wanted me!

In my third year at Cambridge, the issue was a simple but costly one. It concerned a call to China. On the face of it, I was not a very likely candidate since I had no interest or background in mission in general or China in particular. The nearest thing to it had been an odd incident at a prayer meeting one lunchtime. Without saying anything that I remember, an older gentleman, who was sitting in front of me, turned round, placed in my hands a magazine on missionary work in Asia, and then faced the front again. I did not know why he had done that, for I had never spoken to him before. Nothing much seemed to come of it. I do not even know if I read the magazine at all carefully. But in retrospect, it seems to have been the Lord's way of dropping an initial hint.

Some time later, I was admitted to hospital with appendicitis. I took with me a book entitled *A Thousand Miles of Miracle in China*, which was the story of a missionary in China during the Boxer Rebellion in the early 1900s. I am still not clear why I picked that book up as I left for the hospital! I never read any further than the preface, yet that alone spoke to me more than most of the books I have read. The author, giving his reasons for being a missionary in China, used a very simple illustration to make his point. 'If you see ten men carrying a heavy pole,' he asked, 'and nine men are at one end of the pole, and only one at the other, whom do you help?' With China's millions and countless numbers of them passing into eternity without ever hearing the gospel of Christ, it seemed obvious to me that I needed to consider with great honesty the challenge to help the 'one man' – the relatively few who serve China's Church. How many countries such as England or the USA or Korea or Singapore or elsewhere have 'the nine men at the other end of the pole'? How many have a plethora of good churches, so that Christians are spoilt for choice?

While I was recovering from the operation in hospital, I happened to watch a TV programme about the Chinese and what they thought of the British people at that time – around 1963, when China's door was firmly shut to the West. I was very interested in the programme, having just read the preface to the book. To be honest, I had never given much thought at all to the Chinese. I cannot remember ever seeing one in Cambridge in the mid-1960s, nor were 'Chinese takeaways' as common as they are now!

After the book and television programme there came a voice. A nurse, whom I cannot recollect having seen or talked to in the hospital before, came up to my bedside and simply said, 'Have you ever thought of being a missionary to China?' I do not even know if I spoke to her again. Nor have I any idea why she should have said what she did.

As I considered her words, it was as if God said to me, '**It is not her, but Me who is asking you that question**.' It was as though my life were a blank sheet of paper and God, who was in charge of my life, had written the word 'China' on that piece of paper. I knew that God had spoken to me, and never doubted from that day forward that China was to be a major priority in my life.

Before that time, I had never considered following such a path. China had never figured in my thoughts until this small series of three events brought me to the realisation that God was quite clearly directing my thoughts and footsteps to that great nation. A couple of people had been faithful to do what God had prompted them to do. The elderly brother at the prayer meeting in Cambridge had handed me a magazine about Asia. The nurse had confronted me with a straight question. From virtually nowhere, China had been pushed to the very front of my thinking.

That initial call to China occurred almost twenty years before I met the Chens that evening. In the intervening years I had sought to obey the Lord's call. That included ten years as a missionary in Taiwan, from 1969 to 1979, when China was closed. I learned Mandarin Chinese, as did my wife, and ministered widely in churches and student groups in that language. I worked closely with Chinese leaders, serving under them. Now I was ready, under God, for the next step. And that night, with the Chens, the Lord spoke clearly.

The impressions the Chens gave me in their small room made a deep impact on me. I have lived in two worlds since then, based outside of China, first in England, and now in

Asia, yet working, travelling and speaking in the realm of China's Church. Our outside-China world is well served by Bible-teaching ministries, conferences, colleges, books and tapes. The other world, China, is hungry for those ministries, which it so seriously lacks. That inequality impresses and burdens all who touch men and women like the Chens in China today.

'**Be a reporter for us,**' the Chens said. They wanted me simply to show Christians outside of China what the needs are of the many, many believers in China's numerous churches. The Chens and many like them do not have a voice to tell you what their needs are. Most of us have not gone to them, and the vast majority of them cannot come to us. So they need 'reporters' in the middle to try, as best we can, to share faithfully what they are saying.

Some may say that we are wrong to act as such reporters. They say that we should only attend to the voice of the 'official' church leaders in China. Do these 'official' church leaders not speak for China's Church? This is the heart of the problem that the Chens were addressing when they said, 'Some people tell one story, and their voice is heard. But others are telling a different story, and their voice is not being heard.' They are burdened by the fact that they do not have a 'voice', and cannot say what they feel, nor share what they need.[3]

Others argue that nobody can know what is going on in China, that nobody can understand the situation well enough to form a judgement that really represents the Church in China in any significant way. They say that any view other than the official one will be based on the opinions of only a small number of people, and will be insufficient at best and deceptive at worst. China experts do indeed have a saying that you can find proof to substantiate almost any statement you may choose to make about China. The nation is so big and its people so numerous that somewhere and sometime you can find evidence to support anything you choose to say!

There certainly is much diversity in China's Church. There are no evangelical church leaders' annual conferences in China, from which carefully worded documents of accord may emerge! Yet the constant interchange of reports and instructions, from sources both inside and outside China, helps us to establish a composite picture. The evidence that the Chens placed before me that night is manifestly there for those who want to see it. The Chens represented the leaders of a group of churches in Shanghai, the largest city in China. Their views were not those of an irrelevant minority, but of a network of like-minded Christians in different parts of China, not just in Shanghai. Indeed, as the years have passed, the general picture that they shared that night has become clearer and clearer, evidenced over and over again by direct and indirect reports from many parts of China.

The Chens asked me to be **a** reporter, not **the** reporter. That is all I seek to do, relaying to you one voice from China's Church.

When all is said and done (and sometimes there is more said than done about China amongst some believers), the basic facts are both simple and clear. First, the Church in China is growing, and in some areas it is growing with revival intensity. Some have said that it is the fastest-growing Church in the world.

Second, that growth has brought tremendous needs both for pastoral help and for accurate teaching to help prevent error in the Church, as people with scarcely any idea about the Kingdom of the Lord Jesus Christ have been swept into faith in Him. A doctor in northern China told me the story of a recent convert who had engaged in a fierce verbal battle with another person. Words had been exchanged, and no doubt some violent statements were made. When this young believer came to herself and repented before the Lord Jesus, she was so upset, and so keen to show her genuine repentance, that she took decisive action. She cut off her tongue. Why? Someone had told her that you should cut off the member of your body that offends rather than enter into hell with it. We may be horrified at that, but we can also be humbled by her zeal for the Lord. That is typical of China. There is a zeal to obey the Lord with sometimes little idea of what the Bible says about how a Christian should behave. What else can we expect when there are still churches of a thousand people with only a few Bibles and hardly any

Christian teaching books among them? Pastors weep in China when they go to seek for Bibles and books and are told there are none. They know that the needs are so great and the stakes are so high.

Third, many Chinese Christians welcome help from their brothers and sisters in countries outside China. Such help must be under the leadership and direction of the pastors in China, and it must be to serve them, not to carve out some name or spiritual 'empire' for ourselves. But they do so long for us to pray for and serve them, to 'share our bread' with them (Isaiah 58:7), so that they may feed their flocks and thus obey the command of the Lord Jesus. If we have servant hearts, there is much help we can offer the Church in China.

For these reasons the Chens and many others are frustrated by their lack of a voice. Even more than that, they are frustrated by the failure of many believers outside China to understand the need for 'reporters' who will give a wider picture of China's Church scene. Do we not understand, they might ask, that Marxist governments work by controlling the information that comes out of their country on any subject? Truth can be a highly negotiable commodity in China's state-run media. Do we not see that this is the situation that believers in China face too? Will we not listen to them when they say that they would like us to hear their voices, which are not being heard under that system?

Yes, we run risks when we claim to 'report' for them – risks that we misrepresent them or paint a false picture in some way. But if we walk with the Lord and are careful, surely some kind of effort, despite the attendant risks, is better than failing to respond to the cry for help coming from the hearts of our Chinese fellow believers. We must recognise that they too are God's appointed leaders under Jesus, the Head of the Church. That is exactly why we need to hear their voice and respond!

Renguang insisted on seeing me to the bus stop that night as I left his house. I did not want him to, for it seemed to me an unnecessary risk for us to be out at night on the streets of Shanghai together. He did not see it that way. The Chinese are a deeply courteous people, and in traditional Chinese thought the need to *'song'* – to accompany you on your way –

is taken very seriously. You are required to say, *'Bu song, bu song'* ('don't accompany me on my way') to your host, as he stands outside his home or walks away from his house along the road with you as you depart. When he judges he has gone far enough, he will bid you farewell and return to his house, as you go on your way. Renguang was clearly determined to go with me right to the bus stop, in spite of my protestations. Perhaps it was the only way at his disposal to thank me and those like me for caring for the Church in China.

As we stood at the bus stop, suddenly, without any warning, a man in the queue turned and barked a question at him. Looking at me, he snapped at Renguang, 'What does he have to do with you?' Here was the other China, where men and women – even children – watch each other in order to report to the security police, and thus gain favour for themselves. It was the China of accusations, betrayal and the willingness to bring massive harm to another for national or personal ends.

Renguang was not caught out. He had obviously been in that kind of situation before. He simply responded, 'He is a friend of my Father.' To the other man, in the early 1980s, a time when foreigners were beginning to come more frequently to China and the Chinese had begun to travel abroad again, that seemed satisfactory. Obviously, he assumed that I had met Renguang's father in the West, or that I had met him professionally in another city. But I knew what Renguang really meant – that in Christ Jesus there is no East or West, there are no Chinese or Americans or Singaporeans or Malaysians or Indonesians or Australians or New Zealanders or British. There are only those who know and love Jesus, those who have received Him as Saviour and Lord – and, on the other hand, those who have not. The only distinction is whether we know and love the Lord Jesus Christ or not. Race, nationality, colour and background mean nothing in those divine and ultimate terms. Renguang was acknowledging a relationship that will last for eternity, as we go to be together with Jesus and dwell for ever with our common Father – our heavenly Father God. The blood of Jesus has cleansed us from sin and the new life of God is within us, whether we are Chinese or not.

At any rate, the questioner seemed satisfied, and the incident passed harmlessly. The bus came, I boarded it and was carried on towards my hotel. I glanced behind at Renguang, sad at leaving him, as we pulled out into the traffic. I have never seen him since. I have simply sought to be faithful to him, relaying to others his requests for literature. And now I am again seeking to be faithful to him, by relaying to you his request that his voice and that of others like him might be heard by you.

'**Be a reporter for us**.' The words remained with me for the rest of the evening, and for the rest of my time in China. Indeed, they have done so ever since, even to this day.

The passage of time does not seem to make this problem of correct information about China any less serious. It is now many years since I first expressed this commission to be a reporter for some of China's believers, yet there still continues to be much confusion about the true situation of Christianity in China. Some, including prominent Christian leaders in the West, promote a position that suggests that China has real religious freedom, and therefore that persecution is not widespread, that Bibles are readily available through 'legal' avenues, and that no pastors are in prison for their faith. On the other hand, other prominent leaders promote the impression that there is no religious freedom at all, and that Christians are commonly arrested and tortured. Both of these groups have wide access to magazines and other media tools to communicate their conflicting opinions.

This conflict of information has implications that are much more than theoretical. There appears to be widespread evidence that because of it Christians in the US and elsewhere are becoming confused, and are therefore unwilling to respond to the Macedonian call to help the Church in China. Confusion is often the parent of inertia.

The truth, as it often does, lies somewhere between the two extremes. The pastor of the largest house church in a major city of China, who has spent many years in prison for his faith, and has faced recent re-arrest, expressed it like this: 'Religious freedom in China is like a bird that is free in a cage.' In other words, a Chinese citizen is 'free to believe or not believe', just so long as he or she worships in government-approved buildings at government-approved times with government-approved leaders. However, if a Chinese believer operates outside of this 'cage', for example by going out and evangelising the 2.5 million Dong minority people who have no church or teaching the Bible to those under the age of eighteen, then he is subject to arrest, fines, and occasionally even torture. That is the 'cage'. Stay within the confines of the cage, and you are 'free'. A US Christian leader, who is much involved in strategic ministry into China, commented to me, 'I personally know of many who have suffered like this. So the situation is not simplistic. I work primarily with those who do not accept the restrictions of the cage.' There is at least some measure of religious freedom, compared to, for example, North Korea. There has been some real improvement over the last years, with for example the provision of Bibles in some regions. But it is still too limited.[4]

God spoke to me that night in Shanghai, and laid a commission upon me to serve the Christians there by helping others in other lands and other churches to hear their heartcry. My conviction is that the need is as urgent as ever for churches and Christians in the West to understand that there is a voice of God's people in China to which, until now, they have been partly deaf.

Notes

1. The group, led by Mao's wife Jiang Qing, seized power briefly after his death in 1976 and imposed a hard-line government upon China. They were subsequently arrested, tried and imprisoned. See chapter 11 for the historical background to these events.
2. See chapter 11 for further background to Deng's role in modern China.
3. See chapters 12 and 13 for an analysis of the official and unofficial Church in China.
4. See Section B of this book for a fuller analysis of these and related issues.

Chapter 3

The Hidden Power: Praying for China

> *One of the greatest lies of Satan is that we just don't have enough time to pray. ... As soon as we realise that prayer is as important as sleeping, eating and breathing, we will be amazed at how much more time will be available to us for prayer. ... It will take violent dedication to prayer to bring the power of God into our lives. This violent earnestness will be most evident in discipline. We must set priorities for our time. Satan opposes the prayers of God's people more than anything else. Our problem has been we have thought about prayer, read about prayer and even received teaching about prayer, but we just haven't prayed.*
>
> (Pastor Paul Yonggi Cho, of South Korea)

A Chinese pastor has said, 'Many foreign friends ask me how they can help the Chinese Church. I answer them with one word: "Pray!"' Cho's words above and those of this pastor lead us naturally to our first area of response – that of praying for China. In this chapter, we shall look at the challenge to pray, at the effect prayer can have on the nation, and at practical ways of praying for China.

Over the centuries, there have been times across the world when Christians have come together in unusual and united ways to pray for their nation and for other nations, and have seen that prayer usher in a move of God. One example of this which merits our attention occurred in the United States in the mid-nineteenth century when, according to J. Edwin Orr, 'darkness had once more settled over the land'.[1] The country was very divided over the issue of slavery. People were given to making money hand over fist, and therefore forgot God and His individual and corporate standards for their lives. In the face of this crisis, a pastor named Jeremiah Lamphia publicised that he would be holding a prayer meeting in the upper room of his church in Manhattan, New York.

It was hardly an earth-shattering move. Six Christians responded to Lamphia's advertising of that first prayer meeting, out of a population in the city at that time of one million people. Fourteen came to the second meeting; twenty-three to the third. Then, in answer to those first prayers, God began to move. Christians started to meet for prayer every day. Before long they began to spill over to other venues as there were too many believers gathered to pray for the one place to hold. By February, 1858, every church and public building in downtown New York was filled. Indeed, one newspaper editor dispatched a reporter to find out how many people were gathered to pray on that one day. Amazingly enough, prayer meetings had become newsworthy! The reporter came back with the information that in one hour he had visited twelve different prayer meetings and counted 6,100 people praying for the nation. New York experienced a 'landslide of prayer'.

The results were clear. It was reported that shortly after that, ten thousand people a week were being converted in New York. The movement spread throughout New England and beyond. Church bells would call people to pray at 8.00 a.m., midday and 6.00 p.m. The work of God, as it grew and spread, was maintained and continued by prayer. It reached Chicago and people like D.L. Moody. It saw the start of his remarkable forty-year ministry, which, according to the *Encyclopaedia Britannica*, saw one million people ushered into the Kingdom of God over the years. Orr says that out of a US population of some thirty million, one million were converted in one year.

The move of God jumped the Atlantic and spread to Northern Ireland, Scotland, Wales, England, South India and South Africa.

Orr makes two summary comments. First, the revival began in a movement of prayer and was sustained in a movement of prayer. Second, the effect was felt for only forty years. It lasted for a generation, but by the turn of the twentieth century there was the need for a fresh move of God. Such unusual and united prayer under the grace of God will often usher in revival, but each generation has to go back to the place of prayer for itself. How applicable that is to China today. It has seen such a powerful move of God in answer to prayer over the last sixty years. And now, in the face of new challenges, a new movement of prayer, both inside and outside of China, is urgently required.

We need to face this challenge. It would be easy for us to slip off into a discussion along the lines of the chicken and the egg. Is it God who has to move first, prompting and anointing us to pray? Or is it we who need to seek Him first? In China I suspect they would take another approach. They would simply get down on their knees and start crying out to God, expecting Him to answer prayer with revival power and to sort out the theological questions later, if He considered it necessary!

John Wesley put it this way: 'God does nothing redemptively in the world – except through prayer.' Selwyn Hughes has observed that whenever God wants to bring His purposes to pass here on earth, He does not act arbitrarily, but He touches the hearts of praying people and then ushers in His purposes across the bridge of prayer. God may be sovereign, but He is not dictatorial. That is why prayer and revival are so inseparably linked. Selwyn Hughes has also commented that he knows of no revival that was not connected in some way with powerful, believing intercessory prayer. Thus when God decides that a spiritual revival is necessary, He seeks to lay a burden of prayer upon the hearts of His children. To do this, He must first find those who are willing to receive that burden.

One person whom God greatly used in China in this respect was a Norwegian missionary called Marie Monsen, who arrived in China in the early years of this century and prayed for nearly twenty years for a revival which began slowly to come in 1927. In her book called *The Awakening*, Miss Monsen documents for us how God first of all brought her into a deep sense of her own need, then gave her a burden to pray for revival, which she perceived was the only answer for herself and for the Church in China. The process began in 1907, when she heard of revival in Korea and set her heart on going there to experience for herself what God was doing. As she prayed for the money to go there, she says that a 'definite word' came instead: 'What you want through that journey you may be given here, where you are, in answer to prayer.' She received that challenge and set herself to pray until she received.

> Having pledged myself, I set out to cross the floor of my room to my place of prayer, in order to pray this prayer of revival for the first time. I had not taken more than two or three steps before I was halted. What then happened can only be described as follows: it was as though a boa constrictor had wound its coils round my body and was squeezing the life out of me. I was terrified. Finally, while gasping for breath, I managed to utter the one word: 'Jesus! Jesus! Jesus!' Each time I groaned out the precious Name, it grew easier to breathe, and in the end the 'serpent' left me. I stood there dazed. The first conscious thought was: 'Then prayer means as much as that, and that my promise should be kept means as much as that.'
>
> That experience helped me to endure through the almost twenty years which were to pass before the first small beginnings of revival were visible. Truly, God works unhurriedly![2]

Meanwhile Miss Monsen studied revival in other parts of the world and concluded that it often took many years of endeavour for missionaries to realise that too great a proportion of their converts had given mental assent only to the gospel. That realisation then led to a 'pressing burden', which caused great distress, leading in turn to the raising up of intercessors at home and on the field, and then revival came. In 1927 there was a dangerous period across China, when the Communists were making advances and the missionary force was largely withdrawn to the relative safety of the coastal cities. That 'great evacuation of missionaries' had a purpose in God's economy. It was then that many found that they were experiencing the same thing – a great sense of personal need and emptiness coupled with a growing desperation for a fresh touch from the Holy Spirit. Those missionaries who had gathered from all over China were thrown together to seek God, then they were scattered again throughout China to continue praying in twos and threes.

Marie Monsen describes probably the most significant experience of what she calls this 'prayer-revival', the precursor to the outpouring which came later, as taking place in Chefoo in north-east China during that period. Missionaries who were praying together then found themselves beginning to put things right between themselves and found that simultaneously their Chinese brethren 'had been visited by the Spirit of God too, and were under conviction of sin.' When the consular authorities allowed the missionaries to return to their stations, the many who had experienced that prayer-revival went back firmly resolved to begin prayer groups among leaders and others to seek God in the same way. 'Even itinerant evangelism was set aside, both by missionaries and Chinese evangelists, in order to make room for this ministry, which had been so neglected and was so essential: prayer in oneness of mind for a revival wrought by the Holy Spirit.' Again the words of Marie Monsen:

> It was an indescribable joy to discover these burden-bearers in prayer scattered throughout the whole of China. This was God's plan, the method of His choice. He needed to have all these fellow-workers with Him rightly related to Himself, before He could send, or we receive, the revival that was a work of the Holy Spirit. The period of waiting and praying brought us to the maturity that was necessary before we could receive God's answer to our prayers.[3]

Leslie Lyall, in his preface to Marie Monsen's book, comments:

And the result? A movement began which swept through the churches of China like a cleansing gale of wind. Chinese and missionaries were all affected. ... Revival was more or less continuous somewhere in China during the early 30s and gave an impetus to the transference of full authority from the missionaries to the churches. Another storm broke in 1937 with the Japanese invasion, but the Church was by now strong and independent enough to come through the ordeal with flying colours. Following the end of the war in 1945 there were several years of remarkable growth and expansion before ... the Communists assumed control of China's government. ... Looking back, it is encouraging to faith to see how God worked in revival at just the right moment in the history of a nation and a Church; and at the right time had His chosen instruments ready for use.[4]

Many of China's prominent church leaders, men like John Sung, Watchman Nee and Wang Mingdao, were saved or revived during that move of God. When the missionaries were forcibly removed, it fell to them to lead their people and take their stand for truth. When all else was removed, it was lessons learned in revival about the all-importance of prayer, among other things, that stood them in good stead.

The place of prayer in the growth of the Chinese Church after the Communist Revolution parallels almost exactly what is described above. The heritage continues. The late Paul Kauffman of Asian Outreach observed that we will never understand why the Chinese Church has grown so much, and still continues to see revival in some areas, until we understand the place of prayer in the corporate and individual lives of Chinese Christians. After 1949, leaders were removed, imprisoned or killed. The Chinese Church saw the forced departure of all the missionaries. Foreigners with a deep love for China could do nothing for her as they watched from abroad – except pray. And pray they did. Church leaders in China, restricted or imprisoned, also could do nothing – except pray. And pray they did. Many in the churches were left with little they could or dared do – except pray. And pray they did. No wonder China is seeing revival today!

The next generation has continued with the same emphasis, so that prayer remains a vital key in the life of the Chinese Church. A Western friend told me how he was driven through the night to speak at some meetings deep in the countryside in China. The rather imperfect vehicle in which they were travelling broke down in the middle of the night, when they were still some way from their destination. The brethren tried to mend it, but were unsuccessful. So they laid hands on it and prayed – and off they went. God had done what man could not, and got the vehicle going again! When they arrived at about 5.00 a.m., my friend was told that he should rest. Many leaders had come, hungry to hear God's Word expounded, and he would be preaching throughout the day. However, his Chinese brethren did not rest. They went off to attend a 5.30 a.m. prayer meeting! The fact that they had just driven through a large part of the night did not seem important to them. They simply believed that they needed to seek the blessing of God in prayer more than they needed to sleep.

Indeed, it has been reported that some Christians in China were asked what their three priorities would be if they could tell Christians outside of China how to help them. Their answer ran along these lines: '**Number One:** *Prayer*; **Number Two:** *Prayer*; **Number Three:** *Prayer*.'* These brothers were making a point! For them there was no other priority than prayer and the need to challenge people about prayer.

Some Chinese Christians regularly give extended time to praying for other areas of the world. They intercede with passion and commitment for their brethren, including those of us in so-called 'free' countries. Given their situation and most urgent needs, that does somewhat put pressure on us to respond in kind!

In the mid–1970s my wife and I became involved with a group of missionaries in Taiwan who would meet regularly every three months for a weekend of prayer, which increasingly turned towards China, especially as the Cultural Revolution was drawing to a close and opportunities began to open up there. The genesis of more than one China ministry came from that small group! From 1980–4, I had the privilege of serving as China Co-ordinator in the UK for the Overseas Missionary Fellowship.[5] In those years I travelled far and wide in the UK, encouraging churches and prayer groups to engage in prayer for all that God was doing in China. The prayer material put out by OMF is still among the best there is. Then in 1984, with the start of Derek Prince Ministries' (DPM) China work, we began to put out prayer material for DPM supporters to pray for the ministry into China. Finally, I launched Chinese Church Support Ministries (CCSM) in the late 1980s and felt compelled to produce material that would inform, challenge and stimulate prayer for China and her Church. CCSM's China Prayer Letter is nearly always the first piece of literature we put in the hands of someone who is interested in knowing more about China and our ministry there.

I am committed to this matter of raising up prayer for China. Knowing something of the intensity of the spiritual warfare over that nation, however, there is always the feeling that it is still not enough. A few months ago, writing the editorial for *China Challenge*, published twice a year, I found myself penning the following:

> Recently, I was meditating on 2 Chronicles 1:7, where God came to the newly crowned Solomon and asked him, 'What shall I give you?' The Lord God was pleased with his answer – because he did not ask for riches, or wealth, or honour or the lives of his enemies nor long life for himself. So God gave him what he asked for – wisdom to govern the people and serve the Lord – and also the long life and riches for which he had not asked! I began to wonder what answer I would give, if the Lord were to ask me that same question? Maybe it would be, 'More prayer, Lord.' By that I mean: more people praying for the ministry and the workers; more with the anointing to pray through until they get an answer; more intercessors; more prayer warriors – and therefore more manifested results of prayer. 'More prayer, Lord.'

But what do we find when we look at the average church in the West, even (and in some ways, especially) the ones that have experienced the most blessing in recent years? The prayer meeting, and especially the **missionary** prayer meeting, if one even exists, is often the least attended meeting in the whole week. Special meetings with a worship group or something similar will be so full that there will be no room to sit down, but only the most 'spiritual' or 'committed' will attend the prayer meeting. With St Paul in another context, one feels like saying, 'Brethren, that should not be so.' If only we believed the words of Yonggi Cho quoted at the start of this chapter, how differently we would act! But we have an enemy who, as Cho has said, 'opposes the prayer of God's people more than anything else.' Satan is not afraid of a church with a 'bless-me' mentality. He will keep us looking inwards if he possibly can. But think what would happen, through any and all of us, if we would only get serious with God in the matter of prayer!

The Bible gives us many reasons why we should pray more. Here, briefly, are four:

1. The example of Jesus. Jesus specifically set time aside to be alone with the Father, even when others clamoured for His ministry. He spent forty days fasting and praying and seeking the face of God and the purposes of God before He began his ministry. Luke 11:1 makes it clear that it was the prayer example of Jesus that inspired the disciples to ask Him to teach them to pray. His prayer was obviously effective.

2. We read in Acts 6:4 that the Early Church saw prayer as their number one priority – they even put it ahead of the teaching of the Word of God.

3. All the other things we ask God for (finance for the ministry, workers for the ministry, etc.) are released through prayer. I remember early in my Christian life reading of a missionary society that was facing complete failure in India. They did the only thing that they could – they went to a mountain and sought God all night. From that point there was a turn around, resulting in over 10,000 people being saved and baptised.

4. The nature of the warfare. Ephesians 6:10–20 and 2 Corinthians 10:3–5 are two passages that teach us about the kind of fight we are in. Prayer is not the only

way of engaging with the spiritual forces we are up against, but it is a major way of doing so. It is our experience that the more we seek to help the Church in China, the more we become aware of this battle.

If you are finding yourself stirred to get involved in this matter of prayer for China, I have some practical steps to suggest:

Step 1
Start taking materials which will update you about prayer needs in China's Church and State. Information is the pathway to passion in prayer, as the Holy Spirit ignites it. This will help you to grow in your burden for China. Conversely, it is almost impossible to pray if you are ignorant of prayer needs. AM/CCSM[6] provides regular monthly prayer letters with general China prayer information and also quarterly prayer tapes to encourage informed prayer for China. Other Christian organisations also have such materials. You may write to us for further details.[7] Perhaps you could introduce the monthly China prayer letter to a praying friend.

Step 2
Set aside a regular part of your prayer time to pray for China. Be disciplined so that you do not only pray for personal needs or for your own church, locality or country. Tithe your prayer time to pray for the nations, including China's millions in your prayer time as well. Do this in your family devotional time, in your cell group and your church prayer meeting. Remember Yonggi Cho's words in that quotation above: 'It will take violent dedication to prayer to bring the power of God into our lives. This violent earnestness will be most evident in discipline. We must set priorities for our time. Satan opposes the prayers of God's people more than anything else.'

Step 3
Consider starting a prayer meeting specifically for China. Set aside times weekly or monthly where the whole meeting is designed to pray for China. Find others who will join together on a regular basis with you to pray. Do not necessarily expect a crowd to show up. Jeremiah Lamphia started with six people

and you may have to settle for that number. Jesus promised us that, *'where two or three are gathered together in My Name, I am there in the midst of them'* (Matthew 18:20). The encouragement of that promise is that it includes any number from two upwards, not just the 10,000 people in the New York prayer meetings of the 1850s. How I long to see such prayer groups in many cities, towns and villages – Christians getting together to pray for China, once a week, once a month, or whenever, on a regular basis. A 24-hour prayer watch is another possible variation of this. This involves people who live in many different time zones praying at set times each day or week with the aim of raising up prayer consecutively twenty-four hours a day. It is said of the city of Wenzhou in China that during the worst of the Cultural Revolution, during the fiercest persecution, they set up a 24-hour prayer chain. Small wonder that today Wenzhou as a city has one of the highest percentages of Christians in China.

Step 4

If you find the Lord laying prayer burdens on you from which you can get no release until you have prayed it through, then you might well be called to the **ministry** of an **intercessor**. I would encourage you to take up that mantle! Intercessors, according to our understanding, are those whom God raises up to provide a spiritual covering for a work and for its workers, and to release His resources through their travail. Every mission organisation and missionary needs committed intercessors, and we are grateful to those who have stood with us in our endeavours for China over the years. In the early 1980s, when we were starting out in new China enterprises, such as radio and the translation and printing of materials for China, there were two groups of ladies in our church who stood with us in a most committed way. I often think that they literally prayed our work into existence! Likewise, when we moved as a family back to Asia and faced spiritual warfare the like of which we had never encountered before, there was one lady who, along with others, stood with us, and encouraged the intercessors alongside her to do the same. The Lord alone knows how much is owed to people like that. When we get our heavenly rewards, we know they will receive theirs right along with us! But the ministry of an intercessor is a lonely and difficult one, and requires the covering and support of others.[8]

Step 5

Some praying Christians are of an adventurous spirit, and they might consider taking this next step – that of joining an intercession team to China. There is nothing like seeing a place to give you a burden for prayer. Read chapter 6 of this book on teams into China, and contact AM/CCSM for details of intercessory trips which visit various parts of China, specifically to wait on God and learn more about how to pray for that nation.

In 1 Timothy 2:1–6, the apostle Paul instructs us to pray for kings and all in authority, for governments and those who rule the nations. That is very applicable to those who govern China. Note that he does say 'for' them – not 'against' them. Division of any kind in a nation, especially that caused by bad government, brings tension, civil strife and other agendas than the gospel. Verse two tells us that He wants nations and peoples – the Christians included – to live peaceful and quiet lives. Peaceful conditions in a nation enable Christians to get on with the job that the Master gave them – preaching the gospel all over their nation. Verse four says that God wants all people to be saved. If the preceding conditions are met, an atmosphere is created and sustained in which God can reach men and women with salvation.

Pray for China according to this scripture, asking that God would sovereignly preserve peace and quiet in the nation, so that Christians might be able to bring in the harvest of needy people. China has a population of over one billion. The vast majority of them are heading for a Christless eternity.

Practical suggestions for specific areas of prayer for China, the nation and the Church, would include some of the following. Only a brief outline is given here, because the best way is to obtain regular monthly prayer material and learn from that updated material as you read it and pray over it.

- **Pray for the nation of China.** This will include the government (both that which is in power today and the future leadership of China, not yet decided). It will also include prayer for the evangelisation of China and the different segments of her society: intellectuals (teachers and students); peasants and workers; Communist Party members; the military; and religious and ethnic minorities. Later chapters contain more details on some of these different groups.

- **Pray for the Church in China**: for Christian leaders and workers; for both the official Church (known as the TSPM – see chapter 12) and the unofficial Church (the so-called house churches – see chapter 13); for the relationship between them; for freedom from persecution (*'Remember those ... who are ill-treated as if you yourselves were suffering'*, Hebrews 13:3 NIV) and for those in prison (*'Remember those in prison as if you were their fellow-prisoners'*, Hebrews 13:3 NIV).

- **Pray especially for children and young people**. They comprise a huge percentage of the population and represent China's future.

This chapter will finish where it began, as we consider again the challenge of that Chinese pastor:

Many foreign friends ask me how they can help the Chinese Church. I answer them with one word: 'Pray!' Pray for the Lord's witness in China, for the new converts all over the country. Pray too for the Lord to raise up new pastors. Lift up the leaders of China in prayer because the hearts of the kings are in the Lord's Hands. And pray for Bibles. May the gospel's door be opened ever wider for the millions in China who still don't know Christ.

Can we ignore such requests?

Notes

1. Source: audio tape by J. Edwin Orr, *The Effects of Unusual, United Prayer*, given at Church On The Way, California, circa 1976.
2. Marie Monsen, *The Awakening – the Revival in China 1927–1937* (OMF Books, 1961), p. 28.
3. Ibid., p. 54.
4. Ibid., p. 21.

5.   OMF, formerly the China Inland Mission, changed its name to reflect the fact that, after missionaries were expelled from China by the Communists, it was necessary to expand the 'field' to include all of south-east Asia.

6.   AM/CCSM here and elsewhere refers to Antioch Missions/Chinese Church Support Ministries. CCSM is the name of the ministry in most countries, except for Singapore, where the International Headquarters is called Antioch Missions. They are the same organisation.

7.   Addresses of the AM/CCSM offices are given at the end of this book. Or you may visit our website, also listed there.

8.   See chapter 14 for more on this 'partnership' between those on the field and those praying and supporting at home. J.O. Fraser drafted his prayer supporters into a 'Prayer Companionship' – 'ten soldiers in prayer standing behind one man on the field' (see *Mountain Rain* by Eileen Fraser Crossman, OMF, 1982, p. 195), while Isobel Kuhn called hers the 'unseen missionaries'!

Chapter 4

Mightier than the Sword:
the Printed Word

> *A Christian teaching book is like a missionary in China. It goes from person to person to person. Each one reads it and hands it on. It is never thrown away – unless the security police manage to intercept it.*

Few statements sum up so succinctly the urgency and value of the ministry of providing Christian literature for China. The source was a Mainland Chinese sister who, with her husband, has served with us for a decade in the China ministry. Her comments are not theoretical – her life has demonstrated her commitment to feeding the Church in China with the Word of God. She has been intimately involved in the production of over a million books for the Church in China. And she has visited groups and house churches in China over and over again, to ascertain their needs and learn how best to help them.

A decade into this co-operation together, her commitment and her vision for that work remain the same. She knows of the enormous hunger for teaching from the Word of God, the millions of new believers who have so very little and hunger for so much of God's truth. She knows also of the opposition by the Chinese authorities to this ministry – because they fear the growth of the Church.

One of AM/CCSM's leaders led a team of Christians from outside of China to take books into western China. This area of China had had no supplies of Christian books for over three years. The team was met by a young girl who had travelled for over thirty hours by hard-seat train to meet them. She had a further ten hours to travel by road with the books to get them to her village, including having to negotiate several road checks before she reached her destination. She was prepared to do this because she loved the Lord and wanted to see His people established in the Word of God. All of that meant a forty-hour journey involving personal danger – 'just' to collect Christian books. Are we willing to accept that this is still representative of the hunger, and the need, in China today for the Word of God?

As the team approached this young Chinese friend, she saw the heavy bags that they were carrying, full of books. All she could say was, 'Thank you, thank you!' On this trip they had taken eleven cases and bags of different books. She was no more than five feet tall. She looked as though she weighed no more than one of the bags that the team had taken for her. But by faith in the Lord she was big, strong and capable of anything! As these Christians from several different lands and cultures came together before the Lord in prayer, tears flowed down her cheeks. She said: 'My heart is so full of the Lord.' After a short time of prayer and some tea, her friends arrived with the truck and the bags were loaded up. Then she was gone.

Another such person in central China summed it up very simply: 'The books you bring are more precious than gold to us.' The brother who spoke these words is married to a Westerner, and had his children outside of China before returning there. He knows both East and West. He could choose a very different and much easier lifestyle. But he spent the whole of that day sorting out the books the team had given him, ready to send them to other provinces. He did not even stop to eat, such was his commitment to getting the Word of God to other believers in China.

Some years ago, a Christian organisation was celebrating a special event – the millionth piece of Christian literature that they had given to their beloved brethren in China. In the middle of their celebrations, a godly old Chinese pastor took a teacup and spilt some tea on the dry earth on which he stood. He thanked them for all that they had done – but he asked them to remember that all the Bibles and Christian books they had given up to that point were as a drop of water in a dry and thirsty land.

There is no other area of China ministry where information so differs and debate so rages. We have referred earlier to the confusion caused by the public debate in the Christian media about this issue. One side tells of the work they and others are doing, producing materials 'officially' in China. It is quite unnecessary, they say, to 'smuggle' materials in from the outside, or to move them across China in a clandestine fashion. The other side, however, testifies to the hunger and enormous shortage of materials, and of their work in providing teaching materials by 'unofficial' means. They seem to contradict each other – in public! How confusing it all can be.

There can be a specific 'China' reason for this disagreement. As stated earlier, one of the most fundamental truths about China is that whatever you say about this great country will be true somewhere. There can be devastating floods in one area and total drought in another – both at the same time, both in the same land! A few years ago a Chinese Embassy official commented to me how great the difference was between the cities and the countryside. They could be different worlds. So both sides of an argument can be true in China – depending on where you are and to whom you are talking. Indeed, one of the difficulties in China ministry is the 'instant expert', the one-visit Christian tourist, who, on the basis of one or two conversations, becomes the local expert upon returning to his country!

There is also a deeper reason for this difference of analysis in the matter of the need – or lack of it – for Bibles and books in China. Most of those who claim that there is no huge shortage of Bibles or teaching books in China work within the official Church's 'bird-cage'.[1] Some of these groups do excellent work, producing large numbers of Bibles and Christian teaching materials. They are given relatively open channels to distribute these materials. However, though they may even claim to distribute to the unofficial Church, and may to some extent succeed in that, they still have to function under certain very real restrictions imposed on them by the official Church, known as the Three Self

Patriotic Movement (TSPM).[2] Those who serve the house churches more directly, on the other hand, function very much within the context mentioned above – 'a Christian teaching book is like a missionary in China.' They see the enormous hunger for teaching amongst those they work with, and they see what risks these believers are prepared to take to feed their flock.

One of the areas, strangely enough, of real agreement between the Chinese government-controlled TSPM and the house church leaders is just here – in the danger of heresy and error amongst China's vast numbers of untaught Christians. The government sees the potential danger of some sub-Christian uprising led by an untaught and deviate 'messianic figure', as happened in the Taiping Rebellion.[3] The house church leaders' concerns obviously are more biblically orientated. But at least both agree on the danger of having huge numbers of untaught believers in China. Passion for God without a real understanding of His Word can be a volatile mix.

The undeniable fact is that there is a desperate shortage of Bibles and Christian literature in some parts of China. The TSPM has given the impression in some circles that Bibles and other Christian foundational materials from outside of China are no longer needed. That simply is not accurate. Report after report from the house churches speaks of the urgent need for materials of every kind.

Letters received from China give some indication of this need. It brings us back to the question of which voice we are hearing – indeed it raises the issue of whether we are hearing more than the officially processed 'voice'. Do we hear the heartcry of the majority of the believers in China who have no voice?

It is God who gives us strength. We lack preachers. The Christians are new babes in Christ. Bibles are insufficient. Many are copied by hand. Without spiritual materials the ministry is very difficult. Many Scripture passages need to be understood. I pray that you would increase our spiritual materials to help us in our study of the Bible.

▓ Our spiritual lives are still childish and dry, urgently needing a lot of spiritual food and nourishment. We request that you send us books and teaching materials.

▓ We are still very far from being close to our Lord, and are very unclear about the mysteries of the Bible. We still don't have anyone who truly understands these mysteries. We are really lacking! You see how pained we are in our hearts, always longing for the Lord to send spiritual spring and autumn rains to irrigate our thirsty hearts. Please satisfy my spiritual longing, please! I ask you to send me several spiritual books.

▓ Now a lot of young people and intellectuals are seeking to know about the Bible, but they don't understand clearly the Bible basics. They doubt the reality of the Bible and its teaching. So the ministry of Christian literature is very important and is a holy calling. Can you send us some books to give to our co-workers so that they can evangelise more effectively?

This is but a small sample of the type of letters that are constantly received by China ministries. There is such a huge dearth of good Christian literature in China, and the many believers there urge their fellow Christians outside of China to help in meeting this need.

To open up this issue more fully, we need to look at some specific and frequently asked questions.

1. What really is the situation regarding Bibles in China today?

It is claimed in some circles that sufficient Bibles are being printed on the Amity printing press inside China to meet fully the needs of Chinese Christians. The Amity Press in Nanjing is doing an excellent work, in co-operation with the TSPM, producing Bibles in increasing numbers. But simple mathematics tells us this can only be part of the answer.

In its first ten years of production, the Amity Press printed about eighteen million Bibles. Yet there are at least sixty million Christians in China. That still leaves over forty million of them without a Bible. And what about all those new Christians each year? Let us suppose that one million Bibles are carried into China each year from the outside and that Amity produces three million each year inside China. That would mean a total of four million new Bibles for China each year. At that rate it would take ten to fifteen years to supply just the existing believers with one Bible each. It certainly would not provide for the 20,000 new believers each day (or 7,000,000 a year)[4] who will also need a Bible.

Looking at the problem another way, if the Amity Press supply of Bibles were to be used exclusively for the needs of the new believers each year, there would still be an increase each year of several million who could not obtain a copy. Whichever way the problem is considered, the demand still outstrips the supply.

Then there are the billion or more unbelieving Chinese. Should they not have the right to read the Word of God if they wish to? On one occasion one of our teams had already delivered all the bags of Christian books to believers in China and was travelling back to Hong Kong. They had with them some bilingual New Testaments. They had kept these in reserve for opportunities arising from talking and sharing with people on the train. Some of the team members met in one of the compartments and started quietly singing worship songs. Soon a man came to ask what they were singing, and the team invited him to sit and talk. They quickly had the chance to witness to him. They then discovered that he was a member of the PSB, the Chinese police. Imagine their joy and surprise that he was so open and that he accepted one of the New Testaments as a gift.

In another compartment some more team members were witnessing to another policeman and giving him a New Testament. Team members were witnessing to anybody who wanted to talk and gave out many New Testaments to everyone who wanted them – including policemen, train attendants and even a man who admitted working on the black market! All over China there are men and women like that, who, as the Lord touches them, may genuinely want to read the Word of God. Are we to deny them that right?

Another largely un-served segment is the minority peoples in China, who also need the Scriptures in their own languages. What about the Tibetans, the Yi, the Uighurs and the other fifty-two minority peoples? Amity is doing a good work for a few of them, but there are many others that are largely without resources in their own languages.

Many of the Bibles that are printed do not reach the hands of those who are most desperate for them. It is true that in the larger cities, where there are one or more TSPM churches, Christians can buy Bibles from the church. Yet in some rural areas, where Christianity is growing at the fastest rate, several hundred believers may still share one Bible.

It is very hard to imagine just how difficult it is for many Chinese Christians to obtain a Bible. Just think what a relatively simple task it is for anyone in the West to buy a copy. It might involve the inconvenience of a car journey to the centre of their town or city to the nearest bookshop. That might be the greatest obstacle they have to overcome. It is doubtful if the cost would be a great problem, as there are so many versions available at reasonable prices. There is certainly no risk involved. At the very most, it will entail crossing the road in busy traffic! It is a minor task for most of us, involving very little effort, time or money. Indeed, for the electronically wired Christian a Bible may just be a few clicks away on an internet bookshop! We would not even have to leave our desk to order one – whichever one we might choose.

For a Chinese believer, the story is completely different. Simply getting hold of a copy of God's Word can mean travelling for several days and putting oneself at risk, as in the example given earlier in this chapter. In many churches there are just not enough Bibles to go round. It is normal for the believers to share the Scriptures, but this does hinder spiritual growth, as they are not able to study as regularly as they would like. Imagine how rarely you would see a Bible if you were sharing it with several others!

It is also regrettable in today's China that some house church members do not wish to obtain any copies of the Bible from TSPM sources. They are afraid their names will be registered and later used by the police to discover and close down their house churches. They sometimes prefer to send a member of their congregation to one of the larger cities, where they can contact someone who receives Bibles from abroad. A collection will be taken up from all the believers to pay for travel and other expenses. There will be sacrificial giving on the part of all concerned. The member chosen to go and obtain the Bibles will set out for the city, which can be two or more days' train journey away, days spent sitting on a hard wooden train seat with nowhere to sleep.

It may be the first time that Christian has left his home village. Once he reaches the city, he may well feel intimidated by the hustle and bustle of city life. As a complete stranger, he has to search for the contact who, he hopes, will give him the Bibles for which he has come so far. There is certainly no guarantee that he will receive the quantity of Bibles he wishes to obtain, or even that there will be any available at all.

If he does receive the Bibles, he will immediately return to his village, praying that he will be protected during the long train journey and that his mission will not be discovered by the authorities. But the risks will have been worthwhile if he can have the joy of presenting the newly obtained copies of God's Word to the pastors and members of his church. There will be great rejoicing, and sometimes tears will be shed for joy at being able to help more believers obtain a copy of the Bible.

However, even when the mission is successfully accomplished, the joy can be short lived. Such is the rate of growth in many churches that they will soon be sharing the Bible between many once again. The answer? To make another long, risky, expensive journey to obtain more Bibles from the contact whom they hope will have sufficient quantities from abroad to be able to meet their need. It is possible their contact may himself, in the meantime, have been arrested or the 'safe house' compromised.

Such a situation of need is common among the house churches, and even some TSPM churches, today. In 1997, I visited a city in North Central China that I know well. I was introduced to an elderly Christian lady, who works in the medical profession. As soon as we were alone, she began to ask if I could help her church – which was an official TSPM church – to get Bibles. She even pressed me to work with her to establish a local Bible printing press! In another village, about eighty people came to know the Lord, but had only three Bibles between them. They took it in turns to read a copy, but between their all-too-rare turns they would write down every verse that the preacher quoted, in order to learn God's Word more quickly.

In another area, believers had to resort to hand-copying the Bible. There were 60,000 believers in the district, with only six reference Bibles between them. These Bibles were thirty years old and written in the old script, which many found very difficult to understand. People took it in turns to borrow a Bible and copy the Scriptures by hand every day, often working so long that their fingers were swollen.

One incident that sticks in my mind occurred in a major city of China. We were sharing with a godly old house church pastor. He told us, in the course of our talking, that he had lost his cross-reference Bible – a very valuable preaching tool, so this was a major loss to this dear servant of God. The Chinese expression for a cross-reference Bible is a 'string of pearls Bible'. This brother, like many others, saw it as having the same value as a real string of pearls! The way he lost the Bible was fascinating. He put it down on a table in the church after preaching, and it was stolen – with the thief leaving his (or her) scruffy, old 'ordinary' Bible behind in its place. We may not agree with the ethics, but at least it shows a hunger! Imagine our joy at being able to come next day with several new cross-reference Bibles that we had just brought in from Hong Kong! What a privilege it was to serve this old man of God in such a special way!

In southern China, I heard a most encouraging story from a house church pastor, showing how God can bless and use even the most unlikely plans. Farmers with paddy fields near the sea one day found that bags of books had been washed up on the shore. They were not especially interested in the contents, and possibly assumed that they might be political propaganda. In any case they thought of a good use for the books, which were sealed tightly in plastic bags and had obviously floated in on the tide. The farmers used them as building blocks to build up the banks of their paddy fields!

So it might have remained, except that a Christian happened to be visiting a friend in the fields one day. He apparently trod on one of the bags by accident, and being of a curious nature, investigated it. Imagine his amazement to find these piles of Bibles, mostly still in good condition, wrapped as they were in the watertight bags in which they had floated onto the beach. A small commercial deal was quickly arranged – the farmers wanted some recompense for the damage to their paddy field walls caused by the removal of the Bible 'blocks'!

But there was more to come. The house church pastor informed me, with joy in his heart, that the Bibles were no longer in the area. They had been distributed to needier areas in different parts of China!

Such is the power of God's Word. Such is the need. Such is the opportunity for Christians outside of China to help their brethren inside. Again and again, through letters and personal meetings like those mentioned above, we hear of the need for Bibles in China.

2. What about other forms of Christian literature – foundational teaching materials, concordances, apologetic materials, etc.?

Over the last few years, the requests from various house church groups have focused as much on the need for teaching materials about the Bible as they have on Bibles themselves. This is not because the Chinese believers are moving away from accepting the authority of Scripture. It is simply that they experience great pressures from a lack of training and the threat of heresy.

Between Antioch Missions/Chinese Church Support Ministries and Derek Prince Ministries' (DPM) China outreach, we have been much involved for a number of years in helping to provide such training materials. This has involved translating key Christian books into Chinese and publishing them for China in special compact editions. The two ministries combined have already produced more than three million teaching books for China, comprising many books from Derek's anointed teaching and that of various other Bible teachers. All these are given away free of charge. This is no passing fancy for us. It is a major commitment to serve the Church in China, at their specific request. We are involved because God spoke to me several years ago of the need to take such foundational materials into China. Indeed at one point a few years ago the Lord called us back clearly and sharply to this mandate, when we had over-extended in other areas of China ministry. It is a major part of His commission to us.

That need has been confirmed by the letters we receive asking for further copies of the books AM/CCSM and DPM have produced:

> ▨ I do not know whether you have *Foundations of Christian Doctrine* there. Recently a Christian friend lent me the book and it is wonderful.
>
> ▨ We are still weak in spirit, so we are asking you please send us the following books again: *Six in One*[5] and *Abundant Life*.
>
> ▨ I hope very much you can send us some more Christian books – the more the better!

One of our co-workers in Hong Kong told us, 'Wherever I have been, there are always people writing to ask for our books, books like the *Foundation Series*. We have just finished distributing 20,000. Now more people are asking for copies.'

Revival, if it is to continue to grow and spread, must see the work of the Spirit of God rooted in the Bible. What an investment we can make in China today, where the Spirit of God is working so powerfully!

3. Do the materials do any good once they are taken into China?

According to reports and letters from China, the answer is a definite 'yes':

■ At the moment, we are using [Derek Prince's] *Self Study Bible Course* as a foundation course with a number of young believers. Both we and they are finding it an excellent resource. I know many are being built up through these studies.

■ Dear Brothers and Sisters, our hearts have been truly touched by the books you gave us. You are certainly workers that need not be ashamed in God's sight. We have been Christians for several years, but we didn't know the real truth and pure message of the gospel. Sometimes we were confused by heretical beliefs. After we read *Six in One*, we learned true biblical teaching and principles. We finally woke up and now want to turn our steps to Jesus who is the only true God. You have done a lot for the Chinese people and the house churches, and we believe, 'Give and it will be given to you. A good measure, pressed down, shaken together and running over, will be poured into your lap. For with the measure you use, it will be measured to you.'

■ Thank you very much for bringing me the spiritual books. They help me to grow spiritually. We all feel that the authors of these Christian books are well established in God and are much deeper in their spiritual lives than we are. The things they have written are revelations from God's Word for us.

■ Dear Brothers and Sisters, thank God I received the books *Extravagant Love*, *Covenant and the Kingdom* and *Faith to Live By*. Thank you that you have helped me to believe in and love God, as well as have an intense desire to follow the truth of His Word. Your literature helped me to turn from being a cold-hearted individual into a warm-hearted lover of God. My heart is on fire because I actually believe that God listens, sympathises and bestows His grace on me when I pray.

Bibles and Christian teaching books taken into China by couriers have been one of the key aspects in the spread of revival, particularly in rural areas. The books are often distributed over a very wide area within days of being taken over the border. In one district, itinerant evangelists visited a village that had 300 believers. They had only a little literature with them, but gave the believers what they had – a few Bibles. They returned less than a year later to find that the number of believers had grown to 800!

Chinese believers are remarkably resourceful in attempting to meet their own needs for teaching materials. One of our leaders met a 73-year-old Chinese evangelist who travelled around from village to village on his bicycle preaching the gospel. This brother carried a burden to teach the Word of God. He related to the leader of our work how he had in the past worked with Gladys Aylward.[6] As he spoke about her, his eyes filled with tears. He wept again as they prayed together. This same tender old man shared that three years earlier he had asked the Lord to teach him to paint. The team were privileged to see his paintings, one of which he gave to them as a gift. This old brother now sells his paintings and puts the money towards buying books, so that he can teach students more about the Lord. But the unmet needs continue to swamp the efforts of those committed and resourceful people.

Responding to their courage and commitment, various China ministries, including AM/CCSM and DPM, are doing all they can, with the limited resources they have, to meet the needs for Christian literature. But the need is so great that the task is too big for any one organisation. Can there ever be enough materials provided for China's Church to feed the spiritual hunger of her believers? It is heartbreaking to know that so many who are relying on Christians outside of China to meet this need will be disappointed because there is simply not enough material available at present.

After a meeting in Henan province a few years ago, a worker from one of the China ministries saw a number of house church leaders come asking for Bibles. Some of them represented groups of a thousand or more believers, but all they could be given was two or three books each. Some wept at that disappointment. How could they pastor their large flocks with so little spiritual nourishment?

There is a relatively open door to supply Christian literature at this time. The present policies of the Chinese government make this possible. The problem is that Christian interest in China from the outside often falls short of positive action. There is a need for many kinds of Christian books: teaching materials for leaders; nurture materials for young Christians; children's materials; evangelistic and apologetic books for a generation that has been taught that science is god and religion is empty, yet who know deep within themselves that it is their own hearts and lives that are empty.

What can you do to help?

I should like to make four practical suggestions:

1. **Pray for this work**. Intercede for those involved in preparing and printing literature and those distributing the materials within China. We have already looked at the subject of prayer in some detail in chapter 3. I shall not elaborate further here, except to observe that wide experience in this area of ministry forces us to conclude that it is one of intense spiritual warfare. It requires much committed prayer.

2. **Give to make it possible for more to be done**. It is a simple fact that nothing limits what we and others can do to produce books for China so much as the single factor of finance. We can go through the process of preparing books for printing (translation, checking, editing, print running and proof-reading), and that in itself is a costly exercise. But even when we have the finished product in our hands, we still cannot actually **print** more copies than we have money for. Derek Prince Ministries has now produced well over two million books for China, and AM/CCSM well over one million, numbering almost forty different titles between the two ministries since we began. These are a mixture of foundational books and evangelistic or nurturing materials, and they represent a huge resource for the Church in China. There are others in the pipeline. However, they will do the

Chinese believers no good whatsoever if we cannot afford to print them and actually deliver the printed copies into their hands!

Although it is not very British to do this, I will give you some financial facts here, which I believe will speak for themselves. Just to keep to our current targets in AM/CCSM, we aim to print 50,000 copies of various titles every two months, and that requires around US$20,000. But that is only the cost of printing. It does not represent the actual cost of the books, which is obviously much higher. To get a book to the point where we are able to print, we need to pay translators and checkers, pay office costs, even the occasional airfare for those involved in running this side of the ministry. It amounts to a huge outlay and our testimony is that, month by month, the Lord provides the funds to reach the targets. And yet – when we look at the need in China, the fact is this: it is never enough! This is the burden which all of us who produce books for China live with. A target of 300,000 books a year may seem like a lot to us, but in the face of so much legitimate need, it is a drop in a bucket!

So I ask you, please, as you are able, help by supporting financially those organisations which produce Christian books for China. In terms of benefiting the most people, granted the 'book as a missionary' equation, it will almost certainly be the most cost-effective contribution you could make.

To make the equation more real to you, you could commit to put 'x' number of books into the hands of believers in China per month. Working on the average of US$1.00 per copy, all costs included, you could think in terms of ten dollars supplying ten copies, and so on. If you contemplate the number of good Christian teaching books you have on your own bookshelf, some of which you may not even read, you might feel even more disposed to help in this way!

Once you have the vision for doing this, there can be all sorts of creative ways of raising money, even if it is beyond budget for you personally or as a church. For example, a few years ago I went to speak at a small church in Singapore. At the end of the service the pastor placed a cheque for S$3000 in my hand that was to be used for China ministry. I was thrilled – and surprised. It did not seem to be the kind of church that could afford to do that. The pastor told me that some of the church members went out on Saturdays and gave their time to raise money for China – collecting paper, plastic and other materials from Singapore's apartments, then selling it on for recycling. By giving of their free time, they were actually fundraising to put teaching books in the hands of the believers in China. Sometimes we feel that we have little personal income to spare. But there are inventive ways of raising that finance – if we will be prepared to give of our time in faith that God will work through us.

Another way to finance printing, which has worked well in the past, is for churches to co-operate with us on book projects for China. This means 'adopting' a book title, either one we suggest or one of their own choosing (perhaps some good teaching materials they themselves have developed). This they can then fund right through from translation to printing, with us doing the work in the middle to produce the finished product. That gives a sense of 'ownership' to the project, and a commitment from that church both to pray and to give (and potentially even to go – on courier trips), so that those specific books can be placed in the hands of Chinese believers. The church members can identify with the project from birth to maturity as they work with us.

A few months after the first edition of this book was written, the telephone in my office rang. A fellow Scot, whom I had never met, was on the line. He asked if he might give to the work of the Lord in China! I was of course delighted. In the end he gave £25,000 for radio and literature to China. As a Scotsman, I know how much that was a work of the Lord! We were able to share that money with at least two other China ministries. It is my prayer that lightning **would** fall twice in the same place – that the second edition would bring in the same response, or more, from other sources!

3. **Go and see the situation for yourself.** Personally carry
    Bibles and other Christian literature into China. Chapter
    6 of this book will discuss that in detail. Such trips have
    so often put a burden and a desire to serve the Church in
    China in the hearts of those who have seen for them-
    selves what is going on.

    Some reading this should ask the Lord if He would
    have them work inside China to be involved in this kind
    of ministry on a longer term basis. It is a difficult calling
    – but a strategic one.

    One of the great blessings for me over the last few
    years has been the co-operation we have experienced
    with other ministries. It has been a changing season,
    where now most of our printing is done inside China.
    God has raised up co-workers both inside and outside of
    our team, to whom the credit belongs, under God, for
    the significant work we have done in this area. I cannot
    name them for security reasons, but the Lord knows who
    they are! They are the heroes and heroines, along with
    our Chinese brothers and sisters. May the Lord reward
    them – and may he also raise up through these pages
    many more workers in this area of the harvest-field.

    The opportunity is there to do something of eternal
    value for China. There will never be enough prayer
    offered up to the throne of God on behalf of those
    involved in this ministry. Nor will there be enough
    finance to produce all the material that is required.
    Couriers are always needed to carry literature in, or
    to transport it from one place to another inside the
    country.

4. If you are bilingual (in Chinese and English) or know
    those who are, **why not offer to help with the transla-
    tion and editing** of material for China? There is a huge
    need for such qualified people to help prepare essential
    teaching materials.

AM/CCSM can advise and help if you would like to become
involved in any of these ways.

Isaiah 58:6–7 tells us of one aspect of the fast that is
pleasing to God:

> *Is this not the fast that I* [God Himself] *have chosen ... to share your bread with the hungry?*

Are you prepared to share your spiritual food with the spiritually hungry? Many, it would seem, are not. Compass Direct, quoting house church leaders, lamented that 'considerably less Christian literature is being brought into south China from Hong Kong. The supply of commentaries and theological books is in no way sufficient to meet the need. There is also a lack of Christian children's books.' The same report said that even house church leaders in Guangzhou, which is only two hours by train from Hong Kong, are worried that fewer Christian organisations are sending in material. Our own recent experience very much confirms that.

One of my favourite letters from China, written a few years ago, serves to sum this up. Try to hear the writer's heart, and let it move your own:

> We are a group of village girls who have turned to Christ for less than a year. We work in the fields and have spare time to study the Bible every day. At night, we go out to preach. The love and strength of God helps us. He guides us when we preach. In just a short period of three to four months, we have set up ten more meeting points in the neighbourhood areas of our village. The farthest one is 90 miles away. As the Holy Spirit works so effectively, the church has been growing very fast. He heals many sick people through our hands. Many are healed just by one sentence. There are almost one hundred people for each meeting point. As the Lord is with us, we have more confidence. We preach at one meeting point every day. Nevertheless, we know we are weak. We have very little biblical knowledge. Please send me a pocket-size Bible with simplified characters.

Can we hear the heartcry of these girls, who in less than a year were responsible for a thousand people coming into the Kingdom? Do you not think they deserve at least what they

are asking for here? Lord, give us a heart to respond gener-
ously, so that such people can have the tools they need to
grow in You and serve You better.

Notes

1. See chapter 2 for the meaning of this expression.
2. See chapter 12 for a fuller description of the TSPM.
3. A peasant movement which almost toppled the Qing Dynasty, led by
    a man claiming to be the brother of Jesus.
4. A conservative estimate. Others would put the daily figure higher.
5. A compilation of six teaching books, used in China, which we were
    asked to reprint in large quantities because of their strategic value.
6. A famous missionary to China. The book *The London Sparrow* and the
    film *Inn of the Sixth Happiness* tell of her life and work.

Chapter 5

'They Forgot to Build the Roof': Christian Radio Ministry to China

In a remote district of China called Pingyu there were thought to be no Christians at all. An itinerant evangelist visited there. Much to his surprise and delight, he found there were a thousand believers. Although overjoyed at what he found, he was somewhat perplexed because, as far as he knew, no one had been in the district to evangelise. When he started asking questions, he found that all of the believers had been converted as a result of listening to gospel broadcasts on the radio.

For years before this, ministries such as Far East Broadcasting Company (FEBC) and Trans World Radio (TWR) had been broadcasting into China, not knowing, or having any means of finding out, what effect their programmes were having. It was the Mao era of Chinese Communism and China was almost totally cut off from the rest of the world behind the so-called Bamboo Curtain. It was too difficult and dangerous for the Chinese listeners to respond. What a venture of faith it was for the Christian radio pioneers during those early years. Was anybody listening? Did anybody care?

But now, years later, each month FEBC receives hundreds of responses to their programmes from within China. Letters repeatedly tell of the value of Christian radio ministry, as Christians are fed, encouraged and strengthened in the Lord. One of FEBC's directors made a very striking analysis of the uniqueness of radio ministry into China. 'Though the Communists have built a bamboo curtain around China,' he said, 'they forgot to build the roof. And radio ministry enters through the roof!'

In 1945, just before the Communist takeover, a Chinese Christian was captivated by the vision of gospel radio reaching his fellow Chinese. He approached the government of the time, the Nationalists, and was given permission to use a small 500-watt station in Shanghai. However, when the Communists came to power, he was labelled an 'enemy of the people' and his Christian radio station was confiscated.

Little did he realise that his vision was soon to be fulfilled from **outside** of China. FEBC, which had also been founded in 1945, had built broadcasting stations in the Philippines, a few hundred miles from the shores of China. In 1946, they sent their first representative to Shanghai to try and obtain franchises for such an undertaking within China, also from the Nationalist Government. Together with the grandson of Hudson Taylor, the representative spent many weeks visiting different government departments, but with no success. The Communist armies were already gaining more and more power, and the authorities understood both the value and the dangers of radio, and were now increasingly reluctant to permit radio stations to be run by private organisations.

With the Communist takeover in 1949 and the retreat of the Nationalist Government to Taiwan, China was cut off from the outside world – except for the voice of radio. No more missionaries were allowed into the country, and those who were still there were soon to be expelled. The Church faced almost unprecedented persecution. Almost every means of bringing the gospel to the Chinese people was blocked. But in God's providence, the age of radio had come. The first overseas Chinese Christian transmission had been broadcast on 29 July 1949, just two months before the Communists seized power. Radio was now virtually the only means by which the preaching of the gospel could be brought from outside China to the unsaved millions and to the needy Christians.

For many years there was very little response to the programmes. Communist censorship became more and more effective. Very few listeners dared to write to the radio station, because of the danger of being found out.

As the years went by, FEBC took a further step of faith. They established a studio and research centre in Hong Kong, in order to gather as much information as possible about the situation in China. Very occasionally they did actually receive a few responses from listeners inside the country. In this way, they were better able to prepare programmes that were tailored to meet the needs of their Chinese listeners.

During the chaotic years of the Cultural Revolution (1966–76), censorship of mail became even tighter. The few letters that did get through described the tragic conditions prevailing at that time. From 1969 to 1978, FEBC received only 177 responses from its listeners in China, an average of eighteen per year. In 1979, after China and the USA had resumed diplomatic relations and the door of China had swung slightly wider, 3,071 letters were received.

In recent years, the total number of letters has been over 13,000 a year, indicating just how much of an impact gospel radio continues to have on China. Bear in mind that many listeners never write. FEBC noticed an almost total absence of responses from one area. Yet they later discovered that the reason was not that people did not listen – in fact many did. It was because the church leaders advised the believers not to write, because it was too dangerous. Listeners from other areas do write, but their letters are intercepted and never get through. There have been some who have written many times before any of their letters have actually reached the FEBC offices. The responses received, though encouraging enough, cannot fully represent the enormous value of the Christian radio ministries into China.

Radio is a vital way of reaching China's vast population with the gospel. More and more individuals own radios, and it is estimated that 95 per cent of Chinese people listen to the radio. As a population they own a prodigious 250,000,000 radio sets (though that is still only one for every four people!). FEBC's radio broadcasts cover 76 per cent of China's territory, and the network is being expanded. There is evidence of a real spiritual hunger. In the climate of recent years, believers have had more courage to write to the radio stations and express their opinions, thus helping to improve the quality of the programmes that are broadcast. This means that they are able to listen to programmes that are

more suited to their needs and which help them to grow
spiritually.

Letters express thanks, and also indicate the deep hunger
there is in many areas for the Word of God:

> ▨ I listen to your gospel broadcast every afternoon and
> night. Sometimes I have to bring my radio to the field. I
> rely on your broadcast to shepherd the church. This is
> because we do not have any spiritual books. All our
> brothers and sisters are grateful to the Lord for your
> broadcast. They all agree that not a church here can
> explain the Bible in a way as precise as yours.

> ▨ Brothers and sisters in Christ are unable to study in local
> theological seminaries because their educational level is
> not up to par. We shepherd the church by listening to
> gospel broadcasts. There are still many who have never
> heard about the gospel.

> ▨ My father and mother are blind. They accepted Jesus
> during the Cultural Revolution. At that time, everywhere in
> the country was in chaos and people were living in fear.
> Even the blind could not escape criticism. Although Pa and
> Ma were criticised all the day, they did not give up
> listening to your programmes at night. Thank God for the
> gospel broadcast – a means to spread the gospel which no
> one can obstruct.

> ▨ Several months ago, I saved some money to buy a
> portable radio. When I am on my way to work or home,
> I listen to your radio programme. Even when I am having
> lunch, I listen to it for at least half an hour. Surprisingly,
> my earnest attitude has moved some of my colleagues. At
> lunchtime we listen together. When they go back home,
> they continue to listen.

> ▨ In order to listen to your programmes, I saved money
> to buy a radio. I benefited a lot from your programmes.
> I listened and learnt hard day and night without ceasing.
> My parents were so worried that they warned me to take
> rest regularly. However, as I thirst for the Word of God, I

> care not for my health and their advice. Only when I have diligently studied spiritual matters can I nurture the believers.

These letters and many more like them reflect the views of the believers in China who rely on radio messages to help them walk with the Lord. But for those outside China, perhaps new to this kind of ministry, there may be some practical questions. I will answer some of the more obvious ones below.

1. What are the Christian radio ministries into China trying to achieve?

I cannot speak from personal experience of any other radio ministry, but I do know that FEBC has three main objectives in its strategic radio ministry:

(a) Training Christian leaders

Many of China's Christian leaders went through the Cultural Revolution, and though strong in faith, are elderly. Other leaders are young and recently converted. They are very zealous for the Lord, but they often lack any kind of formal, consistent, Bible training. Sometimes Christians with only a few months' experience are asked to take leadership positions in churches. This is not an ideal situation, as it can so easily lead to heresy and false doctrine.

A decade ago a brother in China said to me, 'I have many young people who long to be able to serve Jesus effectively, but I cannot train them because I do not have the personnel or the materials to do so. I cannot send them to the TSPM seminaries, because the content is too political. Nor can I send them abroad, for to do so would mean that their records would be marked.' Radio is one of the ways in which we can help in such situations. Certain radio programmes, even blocks of time at certain stages of the day, are set aside for the specific purpose of training present and future church leaders.

(b) Nurturing new Christians

This is extremely important because of the lack of Bibles and other Christian literature. Groups that have embraced false teaching can so easily lead new converts astray. This is what one new believer wrote to FEBC:

> I converted to Jesus Christ in 1993. I attended a local church on every Sunday evening. But later I was told by some Christians that my church in fact belongs to the Shouters sect. As I also noticed church dissension here, I left and attended a Three-Self church which was quite far from my home. Yet somebody warned me that this church was not led by Christ and their congregation will not have eternal life. I left there then. Recently, a lady invited me to her church. She emphasised that they worship the true God who has come into the world. I am puzzled. Which church is God's body? I dare not go to hers or anywhere else.

In view of the severe shortage of literature, as discussed in the previous chapter, the strategic value of radio cannot be stressed highly enough. For some believers radio broadcasts are the only source of help and spiritual nourishment they receive. For geographical or other reasons, they have no church or pastor, so the broadcasts have to become both to them.

(c) Evangelising the lost

There is huge spiritual hunger in China today. Marxism has failed to meet the deepest needs of the people, and that has left them in a spiritual vacuum. Many are looking for an ideology that will satisfy. As seventy to eighty per cent of the population lives in rural areas, radio is often the only means of reaching them.

Many of the responses FEBC receives come from unbelievers wanting to know more about Jesus. Others come from those who found Christ while listening to the broadcasts.

Each person who writes risks persecution by the authorities, but letters such as those quoted below continue to come in:

> ■ I must thank God for giving me the opportunity to know Him and accept Him as my Saviour through your broadcasts. My attitude towards life has changed and life has become meaningful and valuable to me.
>
> ■ Having listened to your programmes since last year, my spiritual life has grown ... my heart is now full of joy because I have found the greatest hope of life through accepting Christ.
>
> ■ I remember one day I tuned into your broadcast by accident. I was only listening to the news and the popular songs. I am now your faithful listener. Christ Jesus has become most precious to me. As the Lord is my all, I will follow Him for the rest of my life.

These letters require a great deal of follow-up work, and those who undertake this task require much wisdom and strength to get through the heavy workload.

2. What difficulties do the China radio ministries face?

Like any ministry that God is blessing, gospel radio experiences opposition from the enemy of the souls of men and women. Some listeners are persecuted by the authorities for listening to gospel radio broadcasts. One young man wrote:

> I accepted Jesus about one year ago. Formerly I did not have a right concept of God. However, I was gradually drawn to God after listening to your programmes. Several days ago, I was summoned to the police station to write down how I had got to listen to your broadcasts. The policemen emphasised that I had to understand the seriousness of the problem. Then I was asked to swear not to listen to your programmes or write to you any more.

> The Bibles you gave me were confiscated and have not
> been returned.

Another area of difficulty for Christian broadcasting
stations is that of bad reception because of atmospheric
conditions at certain times of the year.

There are problems too in the area of staff and finance.
Skilled workers are needed in various fields – technical and
language skills, responding to letters, programme preparation and so on. Costly equipment is needed to broadcast the
programmes, not to mention the cost of the actual broadcasting.

My own personal involvement in Christian radio ministry to
China began in 1983. I was spending time waiting on the
Lord. As I listened to the Lord, I received unexpected direc-
tions from Him. 'Take Derek Prince into China' were the
instructions I received. At that time, I did not know Derek
Prince personally, but was aware and appreciative of his
ministry and teaching gift. In obedience, I approached Derek
and told him what I felt God was asking me to do. Together
we agreed to investigate in faith the possibility of broadcasting his teaching material into China. When I was next in
Hong Kong, I left some English sample tapes of Derek
Prince's material with FEBC. I then travelled into China on
one of my visits, giving me the right environment to pray
that they would be clear about what God was saying. On my
return to Hong Kong, I learned that FEBC felt it was right to
proceed. Thus I became personally responsible for regular
programmes into China.

It is my view and that of many others that Derek Prince has
a unique teaching gift. When he explains the Word of God
on a particular subject, the listener may feel that what has
been taught is obvious – until he realises that he did not
understand it until Derek opened God's Word to him with
such clarity. At the outbreak of the Second World War, Derek
was a faculty member at King's College, Cambridge. He was
far from God. But God met him, saved him and turned his life
around. He never returned to teach at Cambridge after the

war, though he was pressed by his college to do so. Since that time he has travelled the world, teaching the Word of God.

My role was first to develop a standard process by which the English radio scripts could be prepared for translation and broadcasting into China. That involved considerable work in terms of removal of Western references and generally ensuring accuracy in the finished Chinese product. After several years, I handed this on to other staff members. The Lord latterly provided a Mainland Chinese scholar to take over this side of the work. She was converted while studying in the UK, and has developed this side of the ministry now for a number of years. We have broadcast for over fifteen years, in several dialects, reaching millions of listeners with the Word of God through our two teaching programmes.

The Lord gave success to this radio work. A few years ago I was encouraged by the fact that a house church leader I met in China was well acquainted with the ministry of Ye Guangming (Derek's Chinese name in the broadcasts, meaning 'Clear Light'). I was even more thrilled to discover that he thought Ye Guangming was a Chinese national – so totally had we, with FEBC's help, removed all references to the personal background of this man who attended Eton and Cambridge, served in the British army, and now has a worldwide ministry based in Jerusalem and the USA!

Responses to the programmes continue to be extremely encouraging. Every month we receive letters from China:

> ▓ Dear Brother Ye Guangming. Peace in God! I have been listening to your gospel broadcast since September last year. The *Living Sacrifice* programme broadcast by you is really a great help to me. It helps me to understand a lot of truth and I have come to know our God. Thank you for your help for my spiritual life.

> ▓ Greetings! I have been listening to your programme which I can hear very clearly. I turn on my radio at 6.00 p.m. right on time. Listening to your programme has become a part of my life. For four years I have listened to your programme every day. I even gave up watching TV to do so. The more often I listen, the closer to God I feel. The

more I listen, the deeper I love God. Last Sunday I went to church and there was a young man who listened to your programme and believed in God. He said he had been very vexed and his mind was in a turmoil for a time. One day he turned his radio on and suddenly heard your broadcast. God's love deeply attracted him. He made up his mind to go to church and be baptised and turn to God.

■ Dear Pastor Ye Guangming, you are my teacher and my friend. Your teachings have attracted so many people and many have come to the Lord because of them. I have told more people the exact time of your teachings on the radio.

■ Dear faithful servant of God, Ye Guangming. Greetings in the Lord! Your radio programme has been my companion in life ever since I was blessed by God's calling four years ago. I have read your books including *Self Study Bible Course* and *Faith to Live By* and listened to all the radio programmes. If possible, could you come to China? If you have any church in China where you teach, please let me know, so that we can have further closer contact.

The radio ministry has brought great joy to me. The hand of God has been so clearly on it. It is a real privilege to work with FEBC and to count the staff there as co-labourers and personal friends. They are men and women who have thrown aside other more lucrative opportunities in order to serve the Lord and the Church in China with great skill and dedication. They are worthy of our support and prayer. Countless millions in China are passing into a Christless eternity. Working in this team together, we desire to give those millions the opportunity to hear of the love of God through radio, to be built up in that love through His Word, and, as God calls, to help them to be teachers of others.

There is always room for people to be involved in this important ministry. Gospel radio stations require script-writers who can produce material for China, programme producers, announcers, engineers, administrators and other personnel. And, of course, there is always a need for prayer and finance to support the ongoing work. The opportunities are there for those who are willing to seek God concerning what He might want them to do with their gifts and abilities.

Chapter 6

Journey of a Lifetime: Short-term Teams to China

In 1963, while a student at Cambridge University, I had the opportunity to visit Soviet Russia with an Operation Mobilisation team. We took in Bibles and Christian teaching books, and also some simple duplicating materials to give to the Christians. It was one of the most life-changing experiences that I had ever had. I am so grateful to the Lord and to OM that I had the opportunity at that crossroads point in my life to experience a short-term mission trip. It impacted me enormously in at least three ways.

First, I saw the power of God in my life in ways that I had never seen before. When we passed through the borders of the Soviet Union, needing God to keep our precious cargo of Bibles and other materials hidden from the border guards, He was either there for us or He was not! And He was. It was amazing to see the hand of the Lord on us in ways that would just not have been possible if we had been sitting on a beach somewhere that summer.

Second, I had the privilege of meeting Russian believers – young Christians who risked so much, whose love for Jesus challenged and impacted me. This was the height of the Cold War in Russia, when the penalty for meeting foreigners to receive Christian literature would potentially have been long-term imprisonment. At the end of the day, it was they who faced the real dangers in what we were doing, not us. I was challenged by God. These were people who were really worth serving, for whom it was really worth laying down a part of our lives.

Third, I became a 'World Christian' during that brief period of time in Russia in the early 1960s. While I was amongst these people who were so profoundly different, something clicked, some switch was thrown, from which I have never recovered – nor do I want to! I found there was a world outside of my church life, outside of my country and my ways of doing things. From that time on I wanted to be a part of that wider world – to serve it as Jesus told me I should (Matthew 28:18–20).

I had already received a call from the Lord to missions a few months earlier. But this trip impacted me on an even deeper level. It put flesh and blood on to it.

I went back to the UK, and then, at the end of that summer vacation, to Cambridge. But nothing would ever be the same again. I subsequently made other visits to every Eastern European Communist country except Albania, and I saw the same things again and again. But not one of those trips could ever compare with the impact of that first unique visit. Each trip was valuable. But the first step was a special one.

That was almost four decades ago, and it is still fresh to me. Not just as a memory, or some kind of spiritual scrapbook that I store in the back of my mind. It is fresh in the sense of longing that you, the reader of this book, would go to China, or to some other land, so that what happened to me might happen to you, as the Lord leads you. And that you would never be the same again!

The Lord has enabled us in AM/CCSM to build a fairly developed 'package' in terms of short-term teams and this means that we can offer you different kinds of practical challenges. Four types of teams to China, mostly inter-national in nature, are already established. Others are beginning to come to reality. In this chapter five brief sections will deal in turn with each type of team: literature, orphanage, intercession, 'All-Chinese' and, finally, some other kinds of teams.

We, along with a number of other mission organisations, have a path to make this possible for you today. The purpose of this chapter, then, is not just to inform you about this area of China ministry: it is to challenge you to consider coming on one of the teams. Perhaps a future edition might carry your testimony, like the two below!

> ■ Once over the border, the feeling of joy at this success is something that I hope will stay with me for ever. On top of this, to see the faces of the three brothers we met in Beijing was overwhelming, and one of the most satisfying moments of my twelve years as a Christian. They could not speak English, we could not speak Mandarin, but their faces conveyed everything they wanted to say to us. I remember being struck at that moment by what an incredible privilege it was to be there.
>
> ■ I spent the first day at the orphanage walking around in a state of shock. Having been used to a clinically clean British hospital, at first I could not bring myself to touch anything. However, I soon got used to it and was able to cuddle the children. This is what they needed most, as they have had very little human contact.

Courier teams

- *Purpose*:   To take Bibles and Christian teaching materials into China, or within China from one place to another, in order to supply needy Chinese Christians with the word of life.
- *Regularity and Duration*:   At least three times a year, for two to three weeks.
- *Characteristics*:   International (members drawn from different countries).
- *Requirements*:   Ability to carry reasonably heavy bags with materials in them; willingness to endure long train journeys!

Thousands of Bibles and other Christian books have been produced for China over the last few years, but, as we have seen in chapter 4, the need for Christian literature is still immense. Once the books are translated and printed, they need to be delivered to the Chinese Christians. That gives us a simple, practical way in which we can serve the Chinese Church – to become a 'donkey for Jesus'![1] Teams carry the Word of God across the borders or from one part of China to a more needy area, to make some provision for those eagerly waiting for these supplies.

The basic requirement for a courier is to have a burden for the people of China. No knowledge of Chinese is necessary. You will travel to the Far East and join with others who are involved in this important ministry. A team normally lasts for two or three weeks. Other China ministries can offer longer involvement. Most people are able to make several trips into China during their stay. Teams are always accompanied by an experienced leader, who has travelled into China before on this kind of team. You will receive briefing materials before departure, and normally attend an orientation time in Asia before entering China.

Let one of our AM/CCSM courier team leaders tell you more about what was involved in one of his trips:

We packed the materials and were on our way to China. There were not many people around at the border and we got through without any trouble. We were taking in three full bags each, plus the material we had in our own luggage. The bags were very heavy. We loaded them into a van and drove to the airport. Once at the airport, we had to put all our bags on the scanning machine. They went through with no problem (with a lot of prayer!). That hurdle over, we went to check in our bags. We found we had well over 300 kilos in total weight. We were only allowed 20 kilos each, so we expected to have to pay overweight. I waited for the girl to give me the slip of paper to go and pay, but instead she gave me our boarding cards. We did not have to pay anything. What a miracle! Everybody was astonished, but delighted.

We arrived at our destination and walked across the tarmac to a little building where we collected our bags. Then we were met by our contacts who took the bags, before we were driven to our hotel. We were delighted later to be able to meet some brothers in the town and have coffee together. The next day we returned to Hong Kong.

The following week, we set off for China again. On that occasion we were taking Bibles to be stored at a hotel ready to be taken further into China. The border was not busy and I was called back by the guards to put my briefcase on the scanner. Although it was full of Bibles, it still went through. We met up outside the customs building to find one of the team had been stopped and had had his load taken off him. It was a little disappointing. Still, we carried on and stored the books at the hotel, before returning to Hong Kong.

As we can see in this account, there is usually no risk to the courier. It is almost unheard of for foreigners to be fined or detained if found carrying Christian literature. Even if someone is stopped and deemed to be carrying too much material, he will still almost always be allowed through with a few books, the other books being confiscated and retained by customs officials. These can be reclaimed on leaving China again, providing that the place of exit is the same as that of entry. Anyone unsuccessful at the first crossing can return to Hong Kong, pack up again and enter at another border checkpoint the next day.

Courier work can, however, be demanding and exhausting. You may suffer from jet lag and culture shock. You may travel for many hours by plane, train, boat and bus. You may have to work with people on the same team who are from different cultures and who have different customs. It is not easy, but the spiritual rewards are great.

Courier work is, unfortunately, one of the most contentious areas of China ministry. I find some Christians are victims of what I call the 'China sandwich'. They are caught between two extremes of opinion. The first extreme states that China is experiencing such revival that there is no need for us to go and help in any way. If you have read this far in the book, I hope that you will understand that the opposite is true. It is because China is experiencing such revival that our help is urgently needed to take books and teaching materials which will build up the multitudes of new believers. The other extreme of the 'sandwich' argues that because China is so hostile to Christians, it is far too dangerous for us to risk going there to help the believers. That also is not true. The most recent Chinese law on this matter says:

> Foreigners who enter China may carry religious publications, religious audio-visual material and other religious articles for their own use; when the amount of religious publications, religious audio-visual material and other religious articles brought across the border is greater than for personal use, this matter must be dealt with according to the relevant customs' regulations of China. Religious publications and religious audio-visual products whose contents endanger Chinese society's public interests are banned from entering China.

Elsewhere the regulations state that also banned are publications 'harmful to China's politics, economy, culture and morality'. The question then is whether we consider Bibles and other Christian books as 'harmful' or 'endangering' in this sense. Our answer should be a definite 'no'! God's Word always has a strong influence for good.

Our response to the Chinese Communist authorities should be that of Peter and John in Acts 4:

> *Judge for yourselves whether it is right in God's sight to obey you rather than God.*   (Acts 4:19 NIV)

The Lord commanded us to *'go and make disciples of all nations'*. We cannot obey His command without taking the gospel to the Chinese and providing them with the Word of God to help them grow in their faith and become disciples.

The use of the word 'smuggler' for those who carry in Bibles and Christian literature is not helpful at this period of China's history. The constitutional guarantee of freedom of religion established in China today implies the right of access to sufficient quantities of legitimate spiritual literature. Moreover, the materials taken in are never sold for any profit (which 'smuggling' implies) but rather given away in a manner that is the opposite of smuggling. Nor is it we as foreign Christians who have decided that the Chinese believers need Christian literature. We are responding to continual requests from them to supply Bibles and Christian teaching books. They know the risks involved to them, but they continue to ask us for more. As one of them wrote, 'One of the hardest things about my job is this. After I have planted a church, I have the painful task of telling the newly converted villagers that they may have to wait years before they have a copy of God's Word.' Can we ignore the cries of these faithful and God-fearing Chinese pastors? Courier teams are, at the end of the day, a practical response to an abnormal situation created by the policies of the Chinese authorities.

Many who have been on a courier trip to China say that they will never be the same again. Seeing China for yourself is a life-changing experience. Many couriers return with an increased burden to pray for the country they have seen and the people they have met. A few are determined to return to China to serve on a more long-term basis. Most have been challenged spiritually and have learned to trust the Lord in new ways. But let them speak for themselves:

 It was the first time I had ever been to a Communist country and I was really moved by the people I met in China who have to live under such oppression. Every time we took Bibles across the border, we experienced miracles as God made it possible for us to get through.

 The two weeks in Hong Kong and China were a real experience of how the Lord can use a few to help so many. It was a privilege to help the Chinese and to see the Lord work so many miracles to help us in our work. An unforgettable experience.

 It was awesome to see the mighty power of God at work to guide each and every step of this delivery.

 I found the trip to be very hard and much more stressful than I had thought, but as I look back I can really marvel at how God worked miracles on a daily basis . . . If you could have seen the looks on the faces we blessed, it would break your heart.

▓ Having been numerous times, I have found every trip to be different, but one thing never changes – the faithfulness of our Lord. He calls, He enables and provides every need. Each time He teaches me some new lesson. It is a great privilege to serve our beloved Chinese brethren in this way.

We organise a number of short-term courier trips each year: you can contact AM/CCSM for details. A team usually travels to at least two major cities in China, taking very large loads of literature to the Christians of those places. The books are provided by AM/CCSM and other Christian organisations, but couriers are expected to cover their own expenses. Tourist groups are still the best vehicle for carrying materials to different parts of China.

The hunger to learn more about the Lord Jesus is real. Millions of believers are crying out for Christian literature. All that is needed is those who are willing to go and take the books across the border. Will you take up that challenge? Will you hear the cry of many like this writer from China: 'I am very keen to learn more about the Bible and I cannot do so without spiritual literature. In mainland China, one cannot obtain this literature, even with money.'

Orphanage and mercy trips

- *Purpose*: To work in state welfare homes, alongside local staff, in order to help care for the children and train local staff with special skills for their work.

- *Regularity and Duration*: At least three times a year. Ten days to three weeks.

- *Characteristics:* International (members drawn from different countries).

- *Requirements*: Willingness to care for the children. Some teams require specialised (medical, social work, etc.) members. Others no specific skills.

A powerful way of presenting the gospel in China is by showing God's love through our actions and attitudes.

Where open evangelism is not possible, God's light can shine through acts of mercy, care and love. Preaching the gospel with our lives is a core element of mercy teams. We can bring the gospel to the lost in the same way that Jesus Himself brought the gospel to us – with compassion and a servant heart. Over the past years, many hearts in China have been touched and changed as a result of Christian mercy teams. Lives that declare the love of God open ears to hear of the love of God in the gospel.

Mercy teams usually work in orphanages[2] or welfare homes[3] in China. The nation's one-child policy and the cultural preference for baby boys leads to many girls and handicapped children being left on the street or abandoned at orphanage doorsteps. Only an estimated ten per cent survive the first two weeks of abandonment, and these grow up in deprived conditions. Many are destined to spend the rest of their earthly life living in an institution that regards them as of little or no value and as a burden on the state.

Just as Jesus showed His love for us, we can serve the poorest of the poor in China. Mercy teams can help orphans and other needy people by washing them, cleaning the areas in which they live, providing medical treatment and physio-therapy, arranging operations, and simply by showing that they care. Very simple actions can make a big difference. More than any physical need, these children lack love and the knowledge of God the Father who created them and loves them. Many children have come to a personal knowledge of the Saviour through the care and witness of these teams.

For a Western visitor, arrival in a Chinese orphanage can be something of a harrowing experience. A leader of one mercy team wrote:

> The first few days in the orphanage were a much more shocking experience for the team members than I had thought. We divided our team into three work groups. One group focused on the handicapped children; one focused on maintenance and cleaning; and the others formed a creative music team that went around visiting

the old people and children, teaching them songs and sharing the gospel.

The first two days were spent cleaning up the children as well as their environment. Medical attention was given after the initial clean up. On the third day team members had more time to play with the children and a whole new atmosphere moved into the place. There were no children left in the potty chairs – they were all running around.

The children improved so quickly with just a little attention. One of the most touching experiences was when the elderly people and the healthy children moved into the handicapped section, which they never normally enter. One of the orphanage girls was playing and hugging one of the handicapped children, and said: 'He usually stinks, so I never played with him before.' Now they were all playing together.

A member of another mercy team, a nurse, related her experiences:

China was an indescribable experience. The travelling was exhausting but at the same time exciting. We knew God's Hand was with us protecting us at all times, particularly when one of the team just escaped from a pickpocket.

The severely physically and mentally disabled children flinched from human contact and were lying in foetal positions when we arrived. However, by the time we left, one of them was able to roll over, another was chuckling and others were snatching toys from each other. This was after simple physiotherapy and play sessions.

We were also able to educate the staff on basic hygiene, infant feeding, play and stimulation. They had been washing the little faces of the babies with the same flannel and thus causing the spread of eye infections and colds. We hunted around for antibiotics in China. With one of the team to read the Chinese, another to translate and my medical knowledge, we managed to buy some. This certainly was teamwork! Forty-eight hours of treatment cleared up most of the eye infections.

The staff started keeping the babies cleaner and the nursery teacher started play sessions with the three to five year olds. We were able to teach them Bible stories and sing Christian songs. We paid for operations to be done on some of the children and I was able to witness one of the operations. Another member of the team was able to mend a wheelchair. There was a whole list of things that needed repairing and we did not have time to do them all. It was very hard to leave the children at the end and a large part of my heart has been left in a certain orphanage in China.

God's heart is turned towards these children and His desire is to raise up an army of people who will work on behalf of these 'voiceless' ones, challenging the view that they are of no value and cannot be an asset to society.

The teams usually consist of around ten to fifteen people, some of whom have to be Mandarin Chinese speakers. Team members, who pay their own costs, go to help, to serve and to encourage. Their patience and adaptability are often tested, and the work with the children is both physically and emotionally demanding, but many return again and again.

Given the enormity of the problems the value of these short-term teams is sometimes questioned. AM/CCSM's policy is to take teams on a regular basis into the same welfare homes, so that each team can build upon the work of previous ones, ensuring continuity of progress. Records are kept regarding the children's needs and assistance can be given in training the local staff, who are often not there by choice, are poorly trained and unmotivated. In certain situations, we are able to employ local workers to meet specific needs in the welfare homes.

In principle it is our policy to work through the local authorities, so that team members must agree to guidelines regarding what is and is not acceptable. We aim in the future to provide a long-term presence.

Elsewhere there are also opportunities to work in welfare homes for much longer periods. Over the last few years several organisations have developed quite sophisticated long-term work inside China in this field. They have discovered that a holistic approach often opens doors which, over a period of time, make it possible for the gospel to be shared sensitively, and a long-term strategy developed. Here is an opportunity for Christians from around the world to demonstrate God's love to China's orphaned and abandoned children at one end of the scale and to elderly people who feel they have no more value in life, at the other. Much of what mercy teams can achieve depends on the people who take part in them. Is this an opportunity for you? If you have a willing heart to serve and skills that would benefit the children, ask God if He wants to use you on one of these mercy teams. Contact AM/CCSM for further details of short- and long-term openings.

Intercession teams

- *Purpose*:   To take in teams to intercede for designated areas of China and for the people there, specifically minority groups.

- *Regularity and Duration*:   Three times a year. Two to three weeks.

- *Characteristics*:   International (members drawn from different countries).

- *Requirements*:   Willingness to work on a team, accepting the leadership provided, to engage in spiritual warfare – in prayer and personal evangelism.

As you have read earlier in this book, God is moving powerfully in many cities and provinces of China, with thousands of Chinese being saved every day. However, this is not the case in all regions of China. Some provinces are still very much strongholds of the enemy with little or no Christian presence. Minority groups scattered throughout China, such as the Hui, Uighur and Tibetans, form part of the two thousand or more people groups throughout the world yet to be significantly reached with the gospel of Jesus Christ.

Jesus made it clear that before anyone could enter a strong man's house and spoil his possessions (men, women and children), he must first bind the strong man (Satan). Jesus Himself spent forty days of fasting and intercession before He began His own ministry amongst the Jews. The apostle Paul reminds us that, *'the weapons of our warfare are not carnal, but mighty in God for pulling down strongholds'* (2 Corinthians 10:4). To attempt to evangelise without first accomplishing a measure of spiritual breakthrough can only lead to frustration and futility.

J.O. Fraser, a missionary to the Lisu people in South-west China in the first half of the twentieth century, to whom I refer elsewhere in this book, experienced this frustration when he laboured for ten years with little or no results. Then he raised up an intercessory group at home to do battle with him in the heavenlies over the towns and villages to which he was called. The results were staggering. After a period of time, in those same villages, there was a real hunger to hear the gospel. Over three thousand gave their lives to Jesus Christ in one short space of time. These Christians were later to stand firm in their faith through the Cultural Revolution, one of the darkest periods in China's history.

Fraser wrote in his journal in the early years of this century, 'I used to think that prayer should have the first place and teaching second. I now feel it would be truer to give prayer the first, second and third places, and teaching the fourth.' He went on to explain:

> The people here are not only ignorant and superstitious – they have a heathen atmosphere all about them. One can actually feel it. We are not dealing with an enemy that fires at the head only – that keeps the mind in ignorance – but with an enemy who uses poison gas attacks which wrap the people round with deadly effect, and yet are impalpable, elusive. What would you think of the folly of the soldier who had fired a gun to kill or drive back poison gas? Nor would it be of any more avail to teach or preach to the Lisu here, while they are held by invisible forces. Poisonous gas cannot be dispersed, I suppose, in any other way than by wind springing up

and dispersing it. Man is powerless. But the breath of God can blow away all those miasmic vapours from the atmosphere of a village, in answer to your prayers.[4]

Almighty God has called on us, His people, to play a part in bringing the people of the earth to Him through prayer and intercession. *'Ask of me,'* He says, *'and I will make the nations your inheritance, the ends of the earth your possession'* (Psalm 2:8 NIV). In recent years, the Lord has called teams of intercessors to go to China with the purpose of praying 'on site' in the areas that have so far been impervious to the gospel, where the spiritual strongholds appear to be the most resistant.[5]

Team members have shared how the Lord has met with them:

> ▨ I was amazed that I could spend so long in prayer. Five hours on one occasion seemed almost like one. I never believed prayer could be so exciting and spiritually rewarding.
>
> ▨ Why should God reveal things to us, if we are not available and willing to follow them through? But as He sees we are serious and willing to be obedient, He will reveal even more. Following this trip I have grown in my faith and in my love for prayer and intercession.

Many of the results accomplished by intercession teams are not evident immediately and will only be revealed in eternity. However, there are times when the Lord chooses to reveal His hand at work through the teams. On one trip, following several hours of worship and intercession for an unreached people group, an intercessory team met with two young men, who had come to a hill to burn joss sticks in order to seek inner peace. As the team engaged them in conversation and answered their questions, each in his own time met Jesus. They threw their joss sticks to the ground and stomped on them, signifying that they no longer needed these to have peace in their hearts. They must have spoken of their experiences straight away, for when the team members were on their way down the hill again, they met with two

Hui people who asked them, 'Where are the little booklets you have to tell us the truth? We heard about them from two young men who were speaking to you earlier in the day.' You can imagine the team's excitement as they had the opportunity to share with these people too about the love of Jesus.

In another city, as an intercession team worshipped and prayed, the Lord gave the leader a vision of a number of the team laying hands upon a building and commanding it to come down in Jesus' Name. The team had no idea where the building was, but they believed it was of major spiritual significance in the city and was obstructing the purposes of God. They felt led to buy some postcards of the city, and to their amazement recognised the building on the first postcard. It turned out to be the Buddhist temple where Buddhism was first established in China. The team then went to this temple and prayed as the Lord had directed. They later discovered that a Christian couple from overseas who were living and working there had been given the same instructions in a dream five years earlier. Who knows how many Christians the Lord has led to do the same thing over the years? One thing is certain: one day the spirit behind that building will fall and God's Kingdom will be established there.

These intercession teams to China are generally of two or three weeks' duration. They often travel to the more remote areas of China where the unreached minority peoples live.[6] What an opportunity for those with a real burden for prayer to go and meet with those for whom they are praying, to intercede for them 'on the spot', and to hear and see what the Lord is doing amongst these people.

AM/CCSM's intercession team leader commented:

> It is our desire to be a part of the increasing awareness among many Christian leaders of the importance of prayer and intercession in the life of any ministry or church. Once this was considered by many sections of the church to be the private domain of certain sisters – perhaps because they were not considered good enough for most other

things. But now God is awakening both men and women of all ages to the importance of this high calling. The prophet Joel's call to 'prepare for war, wake up the mighty men...' is so relevant in this hour. This no doubt includes the mighty women, but many of them have been awake on the front lines of prayer and intercession for many years, so perhaps the 'mighty men' need to heed Joel more on this matter! At times we may labour, struggling in prayer for many days without seeing any results. But that only serves to demonstrate how this prayer ministry, more than most other ministries, is in line with the Word of God – *'not by might, nor by power, but by my Spirit, says the Lord.'*

Could the Lord be calling you to join one of these teams and feel more of His heart for the people of China? Again contact AM/CCSM for further information.

All-Chinese teams

- **Purpose**:   Ethnic Chinese from outside of China (Singapore, Malaysia, UK, Australia, USA, etc.) who travel into China in teams to teach Christian leaders and other Christians or to work with students.

- **Regularity and Duration**:   At least three times a year. About two weeks in length.

- **Characteristics**:   Must be ethnic Chinese from outside of China; must speak at least some Chinese – or be willing to learn quickly!

- **Requirements**:   Willingness to work in teams; willingness to live with and minister to local believers (conditions can be basic); ability to teach the Word of God, or lead discussion following the preaching of the Word, and to share personal testimony.

One of the most urgent needs of the Church in China today is for strong teaching in the Word of God and discipleship for its leaders. Given the kind of church growth I describe in other places in this book,[7] the need for training and equipping pastors and teachers to be able to disciple the believers under their care cannot be overestimated. Many have been thrust into spiritual leadership positions within a very short space of time after their own salvation, and have had next to no training to help them carry out their responsibilities. It is small wonder then that many leaders find themselves severely handicapped in their efforts to pastor their flocks. Others in Christian leadership continue to struggle with sin in their own lives, which prevents them from fully becoming what God intends them to be for His Church. Or they may be held in bondage to the past because of suffering and persecution – perhaps even betrayal by fellow Christians. Those from outside may not have any real understanding of what the Christians in China have been through in the not-so-distant past, but the Holy Spirit can still use them to bring healing and deliverance through teaching of the Word and prayer ministry that follows from the application of the Word of God.

Experience in China ministry has shown us that teams composed of ethnic Chinese Christians are able to work much 'closer to the ground' than can Caucasians or other ethnic groups. Of course the 'foreign-ness' of men or women from Taiwan or Singapore will quickly become evident if they are subjected to close scrutiny, but to the casual observer they will not stand out. This is especially important where there are opportunities to train pastors or work with Christian student groups. The Chinese authorities are highly sensitive to activities of this sort, which they sometimes view as politically subversive, but this danger is lessened where there is no obviously Western presence.

The All-Chinese Ministry Team concept was birthed to mobilise overseas Chinese Christians to minister to their brethren in China, through teaching the Word of God and ministering in the power and gifts of the Holy Spirit. If you are an ethnic Chinese and you are able to speak Mandarin, I would challenge you with this opportunity. Put what you have learned in your home countries from the preaching of the Word of God and from Christian books and tapes into practice, and see what God can do through you in China. Imagine the joy of knowing that your obedience in going has made a difference to Christian leaders in China, who in this way have come more into their destiny and become more equipped to serve the Lord.

You may ask if you are qualified to go and impart to the Chinese Christians. The Lord will help you as you seek to serve His Church. You will always work in a team and you will not be expected to share what you yourself do not know. It is our intent increasingly to send in with our teams a curriculum on VCD which will give the believers sound doctrinal teaching. The team can then follow this up with discussion and testimony.

One Asian Chinese Christian, who had never dared to share the gospel back home in Singapore, wrote, 'I never thought I could share the gospel with eight university students at once for more than two hours. The Holy Spirit just kept pouring His words through me! I had the boldness that enabled me to speak to them heart to heart; they were so ministered to by those words that they kept me there until the lights went off in their hostel room!'

Another brother, who is an active Bible teacher and pulpit speaker in Singapore, is now open to the Lord to lead him longer term into China. He writes:

> Only in China can I teach the Word of God for three hours each session and for the entire day! Moreover, the Lord gave me words of knowledge and quickened entire sermons to me just moments after arriving at a new preaching point with totally new people that I have not previously met. The people who listen are often gripped with deep conviction of sin and come up openly to confess their sins in repentance. The anointing that the Lord gives me whilst I am in China is so uniquely awesome. I know it is only because the Lord longs so much for more workers to go there for this very ripe and very plentiful harvest.

The AM/CCSM co-worker who currently leads these teams into China describes the impact made on those who take part:

> All testify that as we make ourselves available, the Lord
> does awesome things through us. We find that once more
> our personal walk with Him is revived! As we step forward
> in childlike faith, we experience again that our God is
> indeed alive and He can work His miracles through us!
> What makes the experience all the more awesome is to see
> our Chinese brethren being transformed as the Lord uses
> the team members to minister to them.

He goes on to share testimonies from the many who were helped through one team's visit. One elderly Christian leader poured out his heart the day the team was departing. This surely is an appeal that represents countless other Christian leaders in China:

> We need you to come again soon and strengthen us in the
> Word of God. I have so many new believers under my
> care; but we have only been Christians for less than two
> years! There are many others like me. If only the leaders
> can be strengthened, they can lead many to the Lord.
> How that would help to lead the masses to the Lord!

Another leader, who was battling personal sin in his life, wrote:

> What we need most is to have an intensive training session
> for the leaders of these house groups. There are also many
> issues that leaders face in their ministry, and also amongst
> themselves, about which we need teaching.

Others, who had been trapped in legalism, scepticism, or a bitter and judgemental spirit, wrote:

> Your teaching has truly cleared my doubts about God,
> which I had for so many years. I am so very happy to learn

the truth! I am determined from now on to live a real Christian life!

Yet another testified:

Now I understand how to discern the schemes of the enemy in causing division in our church. I repent for my pride and blindness in judging my sister in Christ. At one stage I was so discouraged and burdened by the things that I saw, that I was totally immobilised. I became lukewarm and cynical. I feel so liberated now that I yield the burdens of the church to our Great Shepherd! I will ask my sister for forgiveness for judging her rather than praying for her.

Teaching on practical Christian living and honest sharing of personal victory over sin, for example in the area of sexual purity, is often much needed. After one meeting in which the holiness of the marriage bed was taught, a brother in the Lord, whose fiancée had been plagued with fear and illness, testified a day later:

I repent of living in sin with my fiancée and commit to keep my marriage bed pure from now on. I now realise that as Christians we are to be different from the society in which we live. Thank the Lord, my fiancée is now totally well! Lord, use me for the extension of Your kingdom! I consecrate my home as a meeting point for Christians!

Let the leader of these teams have the final word:

My prayer is that you will swiftly heed the Lord's call and the appeal of our Chinese brethren. Come, be part of God's awesome work! Do contact AM/CCSM and find out more about our upcoming All-Chinese ministry teams.

Other more specialised teams

(a) Sports teams

- *Purpose*: Teams that play basketball or other sports. The combination of sporting skills and lifestyle witness gives openings for the gospel.
- *Regularity and Duration*:   Irregular.
- *Characteristics*: International (members drawn from different countries).
- *Requirements*: Willingness to use sporting ability for the gospel's sake. Must have genuine basketball or other sporting skills.

(b) Student teams

- *Purpose*: To take teams in to meet with university students, to build relationships, and through this to share the gospel.
- *Regularity and Duration*:   Irregular.
- *Characteristics*: International (members drawn from different countries).
- *Requirements*: Willingness to use the teaching of English, computer, drama, music or other skills for the gospel's sake.

(c) 'Expert' teams

- *Purpose*:   Teams comprised of highly qualified medical or other experts who can lecture and train in medical schools or equivalent workplaces. The combination of professional skills and lifestyle witness gives openings for the gospel.
- *Regularity and Duration*:   Irregular.
- *Characteristics*: International (members drawn from different countries).
- *Requirements*: Willingness to use professional skills for the gospel's sake. Must be highly qualified in the relevant field.

As I said at the beginning of the chapter, it is our heartcry in AM/CCSM that you would take the opportunity to go on a team to China. As one brother wrote:

> In China, although the environment is closed, hearts are so open to receive the good news. All I needed to do was to share the gospel with anyone – the bus drivers, the taxi drivers and passers-by, and they were mostly more than willing to listen and many even ended up accepting the Lord there and then. In Singapore, the environment is so open, but hearts are often so closed. Now I know where I will invest the next three to six years of my life. It is where the returns will be higher.

Another Christian, who runs a successful garment factory in Malaysia, wrote:

> After seeing the spiritual needs in China on the trip, my wife and I are now in the process of winding down our business and moving long term into China. I was especially touched when, by the Lord's divine appointment, I met up with a brother in the Lord that I had known before. I was so moved to find out that he and his wife and children have been based in China doing language studies in preparation to reach an unreached people group.

Coming on one of these teams might be the first step in a whole new direction in your life. On the other hand, it might be that the result of your going on a team would be that the Lord does not change your place of service, but changes you in that place, by putting a new fire in your heart to bring what you have seen and experienced in China into your local church. AM/CCSM trains Christians to be 'representatives' in their local areas and churches. By speaking at small meetings such representatives encourage local Christians to take a first step towards involvement in missions, and that might be to sign up for one of these trips. (If you are interested in knowing more about 'reps', contact one of the offices listed in Appendix 4.)

There is still much that I could say about this area of Christian service. The whole question of the balance between the short-term teams and long-term workers is an important one. Much damage can be done by those who are only focused on quick gain, and sometimes go too public in China, using methods that are inappropriate there. Long-term work in China can be jeopardised by this lack of wisdom. But the golden rule is a simple if brutal one – do what your team leader tells you!

Again, those readers who are ethnic Chinese, and particularly those who are Chinese speaking, are needed on the 'All-Chinese' teams as well as on the mercy, intercession and courier teams. If you are bilingual (English and Chinese speaking) you are an exceptionally valuable commodity, and need perhaps to pray less about whether you should go – rather only about which kind of team you should join!

There are inherent dangers in these teams. Many people and churches nowadays seem to feel they can 'do mission' by using only the short-term approach. As an organisation we are committed to the long-term strategy, which we feel to be the ideal in most situations. However, we also believe most strongly in the value of the short-term, as much as anything, for the impact that the 'China exposure' has on most of those who go on such teams. Paul said that we should use all means for all men, that we might by all means save some (1 Corinthians 9:22), and in our view that most certainly includes short-term teams.

Whether you are old or young, Asian or Western, called to spread the Word of God, to care for children or to prayer, our heartcry is a simple one – that you would carefully consider the challenge of taking this special kind of journey, perhaps using your precious vacation time, and go to serve in China. If you do, you will have the joy of making a difference, however small you feel it might be, in the lives of those you meet. You will see God at work in ways that, within your 'comfort zones' at home, you probably never have.

I think I can guarantee that you too will never be the same again!

Notes

1. 'Donkey' is China ministry slang for one who carries Bibles and Christian materials into China.
2. 'Orphanage' is not a strictly accurate term in that the majority of children in them have been abandoned rather than actually orphaned.
3. 'Welfare homes' differ from 'orphanages' in that they also house elderly people on the same compound.
4. See J.O. Fraser, *The Prayer of Faith* (OMF, 1958).
5. The power of praying in this way (often called 'prayer walking') is becoming well recognised.
6. See chapter 9 for more about China's minority peoples.
7. A fuller understanding of the problems and needs outlined here is given in section B, chapters 11–13.

Chapter 7

Willing Servants:
Christian Professionals in China

Wang asked me one day to tell him more about the Bible. He had listened to the gospel over a period of time, but found it difficult to fully trust in Christ. It was a real struggle for him. He was all alone in a city where he knew no other Christians. Later he told me: 'God is wonderful! What you told me is true!' He had been reading his Bible twice a day and found real encouragement. His friends are now asking about his faith and also for copies of the Bible. He added, 'There were many things I never understood in the Bible before I believed, but now it seems clear. Before, the only living Bible I was reading was you.'

These are the words of a Christian from overseas who, while working professionally in China, was able to befriend Wang and lead him to faith in Christ. The bottom line is a powerful one: because that foreign Christian left the security and comfort of his homeland and went to live in China, his Chinese friend found Jesus. Because he was able to meet a Christian Wang was able to observe the truths he read about in the Bible lived out before him in the life of this foreign Christian.

This chapter aims to inform you about the opportunities that exist today to live and work within China. You will know by now that I want to do more than communicate information: if your personal circumstances are flexible, I also want to challenge you to consider acting on it! The values of short-term teams have been outlined in the previous chapter. But perhaps their greatest value is that they have resulted in some deciding to work long-term in China.

For those who want longer-term, hands-on experience of China, and an opportunity to serve the Chinese people, there are various avenues that can be pursued. There are opportunities for teachers, for men and women with technical, scientific and professional skills of various kinds, and numerous openings for students in various disciplines, especially those who want to learn Chinese. We shall look at each of these three categories in turn, but first some general comments which apply to them all need to be made.

Those who go to serve the people of China must above all be men and women of integrity. A servant attitude is of utmost importance, as is the quality of their personal lifestyle. They will be expected to share their skills and their expertise without being patronising or superior. Moreover, they will need to fit into their environment without constant negative comments about material conditions or China's endless bureaucracy. The difference between Christians and non-Christians is often clearly seen by the Chinese people themselves in our attitudes to matters like these. If the qualities of truth and love stand out, then questions will be asked. Verbal testimony flows naturally out of the witness of a consistent life.

Of course, there are restrictions and any Christian working in China needs to be aware of these. China still has an avowedly Marxist regime, which views everything, including religion, as in some way political. If foreigners do anything too publicly by way of preaching or leading people to faith in Christ, that is going to be viewed as subversive and as hostile to the State. We need to accept the limitations these perceptions pose upon us if we are going to be effective ambassadors for Christ. Patience, dependence on the Holy Spirit's leading and a servant spirit are the qualities that lead to spiritual rewards in such an environment.

To safeguard the precious openings that there may be to serve the Lord, and to avoid compromising others, it will be necessary to adhere to the following guidelines.

First, Christian professionals in China should never distribute gospel literature on an open basis. Marxists know the power of propaganda, having used it to great effect in their 'liberation' campaigns, so they will not tolerate any known or very open attempt to hand out gospel tracts. To be found doing so could quickly lead to expulsion from the country, or at least to increased surveillance by the authorities, both for the person concerned and for those associated with him. Such a lack of wisdom can seriously compromise other Christians, both foreign and local, and jeopardise opportunities for the gospel.

Second, they should not engage in open evangelism or preaching. As I have already said, there will be opportunities that arise for personal witnessing on a one-to-one or small-group basis, but the initiative for that is usually best left to others approaching us, rather than the other way around.

Third, church planting or open involvement with local church activity is not usually wise or desirable, especially in the early years of service in China. It is the era of the indigenous Church in China, and Christians from overseas are there to serve in a hidden and sometimes unrewarded way. There may be wonderful opportunities to teach the Word of God, or to play an instrument in a worship service, as the Lord leads, but these will tend to be the exception rather than the rule. One-to-one sharing, away from the public eye, is the more common avenue.

Fourth, the professional in China should not openly advertise Bible study groups or in any way publicly identify himself or herself as being involved with direct Bible teaching or discipleship. Requests from individuals or families can lead to a sharing of the Scriptures. Small low-profile discipleship groups for key and trusted contacts may be possible, but should have a self-destruct mechanism built into them, so that the young believers can be fed into local churches or other groups.

Fifth, in view of the government restrictions on local church affairs, extreme care needs to be taken in communicating sensitive information by e-mail, regular mail or telephone calls. Foreign churches or prayer groups should be encouraged not to carry such information in open newsletters. Lapses here can lead to problems, even expulsion, for the foreigner, and worse consequences still for the Chinese believers he or she is trying to serve.

Of course, these are guidelines only. The Holy Spirit is not restricted and He can lead into all sorts of wonderful opportunities and there are many stories where that has been so. Furthermore, there are varying degrees of restriction or freedom in China, depending on how 'hard-line' the authorities are in a given area or period of time. Nevertheless, it is better to be prepared for things to be very tight and take care not to take liberties that might seriously affect others. If things turn out to be freer than expected for you, then give thanks for that, but still proceed cautiously.

There are then two extremes to be avoided: paranoia about sharing Jesus at all, or proclaiming our beliefs publicly at every apparent opportunity in the mistaken understanding that this is fulfilling the Great Commission. It is easy to create a negative environment for foreign workers who may come later. It is also easy to get local believers into trouble. There is a time to speak and a time to keep silent: it is important to know the difference.

Any professional who is willing to work within the above limitations, love the people he or she is serving, and show a real concern for them, will be used by God. But God-given discernment must be exercised. China is no place for the headstrong, the self-opinionated or the insensitive. It is a place for those who are teachable and willing to be highly accountable to other foreign or local Chinese believers around them.

Some younger believers in the West have grown up in a generation that very much emphasises their own personal gifts and abilities. China will prove a painful testing ground for some with this kind of background, because there may not be any avenue for them to fulfil their talents and giftings. They may have to lay all their aspirations down, in order to benefit the wider Body of Christ and the longer-term work. It will help such believers to meditate on the fact that indigenous Chinese leaders like Wang Mingdao spent what should have been the best years of their ministry suffering in prison for their faith in Christ. They had to surrender personal fame and ministry fulfilment for their faithfulness to their Lord. It would be absurd if we, in going to serve in China, should expect our path to be easier than theirs.

As we have seen, there is a deep spiritual hunger in the hearts of many in China, and it is relatively easy to get into witnessing situations through personal conversation. Professionals often have contact with fairly important Chinese officials and with future leaders. With the Chinese people, relationships are all important, and their openness increases as trust is built up.

People are allowed into China in professional capacities on the understanding that they are there to do a professional job. It is important to remember that and to be sure to work always to a standard of excellence, as much depends on it. One Chinese educational director put it very succinctly when he said, 'We want devoted teachers.' That sentiment would apply equally to the other categories listed below.

In summary: the most important qualifications for serving as a professional are a call to China, and a desire and willingness to serve and to grow spiritually. Academic qualifications or business and technical skills are obviously essential. But there is no substitute for a servant heart and the right kind of attitude. Whatever profession a Christian practises in China, it must not be used as a disguise. There must be a genuine desire to serve the people of China in their attempt to modernise their nation.

Teachers in China

Perhaps the greatest opportunity at present to serve in China is for those who are able to go and teach for a year or two – or more – in a university or college. In order to raise educational standards and to train a new generation, China must have people with a command of English. Universities and colleges are looking for people from English-speaking countries who are willing to come and help them in this task. Thus the door is wide open for Christian teachers to find a job in China and make an impact on the brightest minds in this fast-developing land. It has to be said, however, that some unbelievers show a commitment that should challenge many qualified believers in the West who are reluctant to surrender their 'comfort zones'.

(a) What qualifications are needed?

A university degree or teaching diploma and/or a qualification in teaching English as a foreign language are normally acceptable. Obviously, higher qualifications make the task of finding a suitable post that much easier, and the salaries may be higher. It is sometimes possible for people without these qualifications to obtain jobs, particularly if they clearly have a natural ability to handle the challenge of a classroom full of Chinese students. Some have gone to China in faith – hopefully having shared the matter with their local church leadership first – and have found that being in the right place at the right time caused the door to open.

Teachers of many disciplines are needed. In some situations it is preferable to be able to teach in Chinese, but this is the exception rather than the rule. Some of the sponsoring organisations recommend a year or two studying the language first. This will depend in part on the length of time the teacher intends to spend in China. The longer the commitment, the more the value in studying the language. Many teachers arrange for a willing, friendly Chinese person to give them some language instruction in their spare time, if they do not want to study full-time. Mandarin Chinese is the language to learn, unless you have a specific calling and desire to work with a minority people. Mandarin is the language of education and government throughout China.

The ages of teachers range from graduates in their early twenties to retired men and women in their sixties. Opportunities for married couples with children are more limited, especially for those with children of school age, but are usually available for those who are prepared to face the added pressures.

Teaching in China does call for people of character and spiritual maturity. Applicants have to go through a fairly rigorous selection procedure, as they must satisfy the standards of physical health, emotional stability and personal discipline. The demands placed upon them in a very different work environment and culture require such personal attributes. It is important that applicants are able to adjust to the cultural differences, and are willing to make a significant contribution to the academic and social life of the university or college.

China is still a developing country. Luxuries that are taken for granted in developed nations may be scarce, if they exist at all, in some remoter areas. This is not true today, however, for the major cities. Most teachers are paid enough to support themselves in China, although additional funds may be required to cover travel costs and any vacation spent outside China.

(b) What does the job involve?

The actual tasks in the classroom vary considerably from one place to another. Foreigners could be asked to give classes in conversational skills, listening comprehension, writing, reading, English and American literature and to help explain Western culture. It is vital that the teacher can generate interest and enthusiasm in the subject. A lively approach is required, as well as consistent attention to developing the students' abilities in various language skills.

(c) What opportunities are there to share your faith?

Some universities prefer Christian foreign teachers to non-Christian ones. This unlikely phenomenon comes from the discernible difference in lifestyle between Christians and non-religious teachers living in China. Some foreign teachers have brought with them elements of a Western lifestyle that are unacceptable to the Chinese authorities – immorality, alcohol problems and a generally negative and hostile attitude to the school authorities. Christians with a good testimony are seen to stand out by contrast. One lady was given the opportunity by the university authorities to address the student body, giving the reasons why she was different from others. When she departed to return to her home country, she left with the request that she send others like herself to work in that university. What a testimony!

Teachers will be meeting daily with groups of students. They have a chance to gain the students' respect through their conscientiousness, the quality of their teaching and their caring attitude. This will often lead to admiration for their moral lifestyle and eventually questions will be asked about their beliefs. These may arise in private conversation or in the classroom, depending on the freedom of expression allowed by the particular university or college. For Christian teachers this is a golden opportunity to attract people to the Lord Jesus and, in some cases, make an indelible impression that can have eternal significance.

Various groups can supply teachers with materials that will help them to explain the meaning of festivals like Christmas and Easter to the Chinese students. Classes have been known to ask openly what these festivals mean, and a carefully presented answer can be a powerful evangelistic tool.

Some Chinese students expect their foreign teacher to be an authority on the Bible, because to them it is an important piece of English literature, which has had considerable influence on Western thinking. It is, therefore, possible to share about Jesus within the classroom situation as long as one is creative and uses wisdom and discernment.

To convey what is possible, even within the restrictions imposed by working in a 'closed country', as China still is in many ways, let me share with you the experience of an American Christian who is currently teaching in China. She writes:

I really tried hard not to come to China with expectations. I had moved countries before. I knew I would get culture shock in China, but I didn't want to have such a rosy picture that it would all crash around my feet. Before I came, I was really challenged by the children of Israel who complained in the wilderness. God was challenging me that, no matter what the conditions were like, I shouldn't complain about the manna – a little like complaining about too much rice. I thought, 'This is what God has here and I'll just accept it.' I should say, if anything, I was more favourably impressed than unimpressed. I live in what I consider to be a beautiful city, close to a river. I'm on a small mountain. The house I live in is an older style one. It's really attractive. I felt the Lord really blessed me with the room He gave me in this house. I just love it and I immediately felt at home here because the surroundings are so pleasant and the room I have to live in is great.

I was hired as an English teacher. I've been given my own class of between 30–35 students to whom I teach all the English subjects. This involves reading, writing, composition, oral English, conversational English and listening comprehension. I see those students around fifteen hours a week and that means that I have a lot of lesson plans to do, as I don't repeat any classes. This is different from a lot of places where you may teach six to ten different classes, but you'll just repeat the same subject matter. But I love this arrangement as I get to spend so much time with the students, and we get to know each other really well. The students become friends by the end of the year, that's what's great. They keep on coming back to see me, even when they have other teachers.

During my first semester I didn't find any opportunities to share my faith. But, then there were things that I just wasn't conscious of. After that I learned that the best opportunity was to use a journal system. As part of the writing course, I have my students keep a journal. They write in the journal two to three times a week. They can write whatever they want. Usually they write about things they're going through; things that are happening at home; things they're thinking or feeling; and every few weeks I take the journals in, and I flip through and read them. I make sure that their writing is OK, and I often comment on the bottom of the page. These journals are totally private. I've promised the girls I'll never show them to anyone else. They're confidential. They know they can trust me with the things they share. I've found so many times that I've been able to write comments in a way that tells them about the Lord. If they have a serious problem, like hating someone, I can talk to them about forgiveness; or if they're feeling lonely or depressed, I can tell them there's Someone who cares about them and knows them better than they know themselves – Someone who created them in the first place. I continually write biblical truths in those journals and encourage the girls. They often write back and say, 'Tell me more about this', or 'I liked what you said', or 'This helped me' – and so I can respond again.

The students aren't encouraged to come to my room, and so I have to make a point of saying, 'I'd really like to talk to you. Why don't you come and see me this afternoon?' Then they will come to my room, and once they're there, I usually take any opportunity I can to bring up the Lord, tell them that He loves them, or whatever fits the situation. I often suggest before the student leaves that I pray with them. I say, 'If that will make you uncomfortable, we won't do it.' I don't want to put any pressure on them. But I've never had a student refuse. Many a time, I've had students burst into tears when I pray for them. They'll say, 'I feel something special in the room.' They don't know it's the Holy Spirit, but they definitely feel something.

I've also started a kind of lending library. I have a lot of books and magazines that are romances, and I also have a lot of Christian romantic novels and books that don't look like Christian stories from the covers, but inside have religious themes and Scripture verses. Books like the Joni Eareckson story and stories about people that God has really met with. The students come and borrow books all the time. They love getting their hands on English books, as the library in the school is pretty bad. They'll often come back and discuss the books that they've read with me and that's another way I can share Christian principles.

Every year I do a unit with the girls on 'love'. We learn idioms like 'swept off her feet', and they really get excited about it. We read all kinds of love stories, and we discuss things like, 'Should you marry for love or for money?' To finish the unit, I always say I'm going to share a poem with them about love, and I give them a copy of 1 Corinthians 13. We discuss it in class and then I have them memorise it. They love memorising the poem. The first year I did that, I dropped a hint that if anyone was interested, I have a copy in Chinese somewhere. About a week later, two girls came to my room and said, 'About that poem you taught us in class, do you think you could find it in

Chinese?' I got out my Chinese Bible and showed them. They took it and read it, and eventually those two girls came to the Lord. It was because they'd been so attracted by the words from the Bible, and it just proved to me that God's Word cannot go out and return void. It's always going to accomplish something.

The general feeling that always comes up with new Christians is that they're really afraid. It seems like they've done something really covert and secretive. I try not to make it seem too hush hush, when they've prayed with me, although it's very important to be careful, and fear is a big thing. For example, I was talking about the two girls before who did become Christians. They knew about each other as they came to the Lord at the same time. But, over the next year two other girls became Christians, and they didn't want anyone else to know. There were four Christians studying in that class, but two of them didn't know about the other two.

If the school found out they had become Christians, the school would try to tell them that they'd made a bad decision, and that they should renounce it and change their mind. Some teachers may give them lower marks, or they may not give them as good a recommendation when they leave school. Information may be recorded in their files which would go to their prospective employer and which could influence their chances of promotion. Sometimes it doesn't matter, but often it can, and they're aware of these things and just want to keep it secret.

If they want to go church, I always give them a choice of whether they'd like to go to an 'underground' church or one of the Three Self churches. I can't usually take them, but I can introduce them to other people who can. So, I stay one step removed. I have gone with them occasionally to the Three Self churches. I've met the student in the church and sat with her, but we haven't walked in and out together, because I would be in trouble with my school. We aren't allowed to take students to church.

Once I shared with a student who was experiencing a terrible family situation. I'd shared about the love of Christ and how He could help her through this. She listened to me and came very close to becoming a Christian, and then just turned around and rejected it, and said she wanted nothing to do with it. I said, 'Okay, I'll just continue to be your friend and pray for you, that's fine', but two years later she wrote a paper in one of her classes that said I'd put terrible pressure on her to become a Christian. I was very nervous about it and I actually don't know what will happen as that student's paper is on file with the school. But, I didn't take it personally. It gave me such an increased burden to pray for her, because I knew this was a student who had heard the truth and rejected it, and I felt she was battling with the Lord. I believe as I keep praying, and if you keep praying with me, that one day she'll turn around and realise that it was the truth she heard, and that she will accept it and come back to the Lord. But, at the moment she just wants to lash out and possibly get me into trouble.

I'm definitely an ordinary person, and China is filled with ordinary people who are simply vessels who are willing to let the Lord work through them. And if He can take my hands and my feet and my mouth and use them every day, that's all that's important. I do have a degree from a university, which is necessary to teach in China, but I don't have a degree in English or a TEFL background, although that's also advisable. Neither do I have an extrovert personality, which is what a lot of people think is really necessary in the classroom. I guess all I can say is that it doesn't really matter what your background is or what your qualifications are. If you're willing to make relationships with Chinese people and let the Lord work through you, that's all that's important.

When I came and saw what other teachers were doing in China, I thought if they can do it, I can too. And I saw the masses of people there are in China. You have no idea how many people are in China until you get here, and you're on a crowded street. You look back and see the faces, and you realise these people have never had a chance to hear that there's a God who made them and who loves them; and unless someone shares that good

> news with them, they're going to a Christless eternity. Just
> being here gives you an opportunity to see the need in a
> greater way, and think, 'If I can come, and if the Lord can
> use me here to save even one person's life, it's worth it.'
> Save a life and disciple someone so that they can reach out
> to someone else. That's the one-by-one principle.

This beautiful testimony is but one example of how God can take an 'ordinary' life – perhaps like yours – which is surrendered to Him, and use it in a most extraordinary way.

There are various avenues for those interested in teaching in China. Short-term opportunities are arranged by some groups for those with specialities such as languages or computers. These are usually of around six weeks' duration and include one week in Hong Kong and several weeks travelling in China. A bigger step might involve an initial contract of one or two years for teaching, renewable by agreement from both sides at the end of that period. A yet longer-term commitment, of at least five years, is also possible. Two years of this would be spent in intensive language study and the other three teaching in China. If finances permit, it might be advantageous to make a short visit to China first to get the feel of the place. This is certainly advisable for someone who is thinking of a long-term commitment. There are some in China today who may be considered genuinely long-term. They have used their 'tent-making' skills in the teaching of English for ten years or more, to enable them to serve the Lord there over a much longer period of time.

There are a number of reputable organisations that have been set up with the specific aim of recruiting qualified Christians to teach in China. The shame is that there are always more openings and requests for teachers than there are qualified Christians willing to take them.[1] Such organisations establish relationships with national, provincial or local educational authorities, who may well know that they are Christian-based foundations, and yet gladly accept the quality teachers they provide.

In the majority of cases it is wisest to go out with such an organisation behind you. One important reason is that the Chinese educational authorities, who are usually working under very limited budgets, may try and extract unreasonably long hours of service from foreigners. This is not malice – it is just an effort to get as much as they can out of you. An organisation behind you to help you negotiate a reasonable contract, as well as assisting in the matter of living conditions, can be a very real help. Sending agencies usually place teachers in teams, to provide support, care and fellowship. These are all very important in China. New teachers would normally be in a situation where other colleagues are working either in the same college, or at the very least, in the same city.

Another reason for going with a support organisation is that it is not easy to live and keep spiritually 'on top' in a culture that is so different. There can sometimes be a hostile Marxist atmosphere. At the very least, you may wake up to patriotic songs blaring at you, an intrusion which is not very conducive to exalted quiet times! You may also grow weary of being watched, with letters being opened, visitors noted, and sometimes unusually direct questions being asked. Your room may be bugged. Then there is the obvious matter of living in another country and culture, where such matters as the food, attitudes and reactions are widely different from our 'norms'. I can remember early in my Taiwan days standing still in a large crowd outside a public building and finding it hard to stay calm when people kept bumping into me in a very un-Western way. An English relative reacted with astonishment at the loud belch which a Chinese friend allowed herself to make after a good meal. What is socially acceptable and even polite for one culture may be a point of unacceptable offence in another, and even differences that were culturally interesting to start with might become quite oppressive after a while.

In such circumstances, some pastoral resource and help can prove essential and reassuring. Sending agencies usually provide orientation courses before the prospective teacher enters China, as well as field conferences, inside or outside of China, during vacation periods. Occasional pastoral visits by qualified personnel may well be available, giving ongoing help in terms of adjustment and spiritual encouragement.

AM/CCSM aims to serve by advising on how to proceed, either with us or by putting suitably qualified Christians in touch with other organisations. Please write to us if you are interested.

Other professionals in China

Opportunities for other professionals are often more limited in terms of contact with the Chinese people. Somebody working in the Diplomatic Corps, for example, may rarely be able to speak with ordinary Chinese people. Journalists might have more contact, but their movements can at times be closely observed. For those with special abilities and economic backing, the possibility of opening a joint venture or some other kind of business exists. Labour is cheap and can be trained.

China will undoubtedly be a growth economy for the foreseeable future, well into the new millennium. There are, however, many difficulties for those attempting business ventures into China. Widespread corruption is one of them, as is the perception that Westerners like nothing better than to give a fortune away to any one of a dozen projects with which they might be presented. Horror stories abound of the investors who found themselves fleeced in China. I person-ally know even of Christian investment projects that went badly wrong because of unreality in the minds of their initiators. The essential question is this: as Christians, could we not see business as another way to **serve** Christ in China? Do we have to go in with a 'get rich quick' mentality, as so many did in the early days, when China first began to open up to the West? We can go in with a co-operative mindset, looking not for short-term profit, but for long-term economic benefit to the community as a whole. We can lay down greed as a motivation and adopt the desire to model Christian integrity instead. China needs to see the principles of honesty, loyalty and trust, as well as shrewdness, demon-strated in the business arena. There may be many difficulties and challenges along this road, but it remains an exciting one. Contact with high officials and business people may arise, along with the possibility of building friendships with them. Long-term relationships, known as *guanxi* in China, are a highly prized commodity and can bear eternal fruit. Besides business, there are also vacancies for professionals in other fields such as commerce, agriculture, urban development, arts, science and technology – and even famine relief and environmental studies.

In the previous chapter, it was observed that there is a **wide open** door in the field of welfare homes, with many attendant openings for those with medical and educational skills. Increasingly there are long-term placements possible in this field. AM/CCSM is involved in a work of this kind in one of the poorest provinces in China. We are using short-term teams to open doors for mercy work amongst an unreached people group.[2] These teams are designed to be a doorway into significant outreach to the target people group. Then the second phase aims to bring together a team of workers who have different skills, but who function well as a team and have a strong desire to reach out to these needy individuals with the love of Jesus. Doctors, rehabilitation specialists, physiotherapists, occupational therapists, nurses, special education teachers, child care workers, nutritionists and others are needed to help in this phase of the work. But there is also a place for those who just have a heart for children and who sense that the Lord is drawing them to this kind of involvement. For the longer-term workers, language study for the first two years is required.

AM/CCSM can help you with enquiries along all these lines. If we ourselves are not particularly involved in the field that interests you, we should be able to put you in touch with other agencies that are. We particularly encourage those who want to investigate these areas of service to write to us at one of the addresses at the end of this book. There are many opportunities for longer-term work, both with us and with other agencies.

Students in China

Foreign students who study at a Chinese university have some of the best opportunities to befriend the Chinese, although situations may differ widely depending on various external factors. Sometimes that will depend on the policy enforced by the local authorities in the school concerned. You may live in a foreigners' compound and all visitors may have to be registered. Local policies may also change to conform to national policies. For example, after the Tiananmen Square massacre in 1989, Chinese students throughout China were expressly warned not to have any contact with foreigners.

In certain situations it is possible to find oneself a little isolated from Chinese students. But generally speaking those restrictions are much less true of the student category than they are of teachers and other professionals. Chinese students are generally of high quality and have a desire to learn, which makes the foreigner in their midst a source of knowledge and potential friendship.

For the foreigner, it is important that he or she enter into genuine friendships with such people, rather than simply seeking to convert them. Harm can be done when 'friends' who do not respond to our agenda are dropped suddenly in favour of other more hopeful targets. Friendship is a vital and traditional quality in China. It is to be treasured. For students there are wonderful opportunities to make lasting and trusting relationships.

One student told of the exciting time she spent in China:

After graduating from university with a degree in language and linguistic science, I spent ten months in China with a Chinese government scholarship. I studied Chinese at a university in northern China. Another Christian who had completed the same degree course was sent to the same university, so it was good to have fellowship from the very beginning of my time there.

It wasn't long, though, before we got to know several other foreign Christians, mainly teachers. Being part of this international fellowship of about fifteen people was a great encouragement. We heard of all the good things God was doing, as well as praying for each other when things weren't going so smoothly.

I lived in the foreign students' block and had classes together with other foreign students, but there were opportunities to meet Chinese students around the campus, especially those who were keen to practise their English. In this way, I became good friends with two Chinese students, one of whom was a believer, although she had never read the Bible or had any fellowship. It was a great privilege to be able to give her a Bible and share fellowship. In fact, a small group of us (two foreigners and three Chinese) ended up meeting for fellowship once a week in one of our rooms in the foreign students' block. In the holidays it was a real joy to visit both of my Chinese friends in their homes, one in another city, the other in a small village of about 1000 inhabitants. It was particularly interesting to experience Chinese village life, vastly different from life in the cities.

It is now two years since I left China, but I still keep in touch with friends there, and I was delighted to hear the news from one friend that there is now a fellowship group that meets in her house. It really was a great joy to be able to serve God in China, even in a very small way. I learnt a lot just by 'experiencing' China for ten months, an experience I would not like to have missed and that I would certainly recommend to others who may be thinking of going to China.

Again, write to AM/CCSM if you would like to know more about organisations that arrange study places in China.

Are you looking for the first step towards long-term involvement in China? A short-term School of Missions might be the answer. It could be that you would welcome the chance to explore more deeply the avenues for service that might be open to you for China – or elsewhere. Or it might be that you feel the need for more equipping before embarking on such a venture. You might like to investigate Marxism, to see where the philosophy fails. Or perhaps you might like to gain the specific Christian skills that are needed in one-to-one Bible study. Whatever your situation, you might like to consider the benefits of attending a short-term training course. Of the courses offered by various missionary organisations and groups, YWAM's Discipleship Training School is possibly the best known.

AM/CCSM offers the Antioch School of Missions (ASM), a three- to five-month course, for those who need time to prepare for entry into China, and have possibly already undertaken longer courses established by other organisations. Based in Singapore, ASM aims to draw candidates from East and West, so it is, in and of itself, a multicultural experience! The intent is to provide an environment where candidates can learn about missions, explore their own gifting, and have practical experience of outreach on one or two short-term teams. The practical side also includes having hands-on exposure to a working missions office, to see the necessity of good administration in any effective work. Issues of cross-cultural living and communication are addressed, and opportunity given to pursue study in any area of personal interest. A strong walk with the Lord is presupposed, but pastoral help and counselling are offered for issues that arise. ASM and other courses like it, especially if they take place in Asia, can help believers to prepare for 'the field' by enabling them to understand their strengths and weaknesses in ways that may not have been so easily apparent in their own lands. I would highly recommend a training course of this kind as an introduction and preparation for Christian service to anyone who plans to serve long-term on the mission field in China or anywhere else in Asia.[3] The essential qualification for service is, however, a willingness to seek God's plan for our lives, to reach the lost, to work as part of a team, and to be teachable.

Many years ago, one of the first foreign Christians in China wrote home and issued a clear challenge: '**Give up your small ambitions and come to China**.' For all the three categories listed in this chapter – teachers, other professionals and students – China offers fascinating and challenging prospects. They are the more challenging when we consider the 'small ambitions' that consume so many believers in the materialistic West today. Are our aspirations really that important in the face of China's call to us today and in the face of the price that Jesus paid for us – and for more than a billion Chinese – on the cross?

Notes

1. All the agencies we know are saying they could place far more people inside China than are coming forward to offer themselves. Some say the ratio of openings to people available is 5:1!
2. See chapter 9 for a definition and expansion of this term, especially as relating to China.
3. For any who feel drawn to work with AM/CCSM long term, attending ASM is a prerequisite. It is 'the gateway to the ministry' to share core values and flesh out the mission statement.

Chapter 8

Strangers in our Land: Witness to Mainland Chinese Overseas

While I was in the UK, I had an opportunity to fellowship face to face with Professor Zhou. I had first met him several years before, also in the UK, when he had been studying in England. Now we had another opportunity to be together. He talked of many things, enjoying friendship and fellowship together. It was nearly time to go our own ways, when I suggested that we might pray together. I led off in Mandarin, thanking the Lord for His work in Brother Zhou's life, and asking His blessing on the days to come after he returned to China. Suddenly I found that he was weeping. I did not have to ask why. I knew that he has very little fellowship in China. As an intellectual he could still face real dangers if he were to be open about his faith. The opportunity to pray together in Chinese with a trusted brother in the Lord was clearly so unusual for him that it touched the deep wound of spiritual loneliness within him.

His story was interesting. He had heard about Christianity over the radio while he was in China – probably through the Far East Broadcasting Company or Trans World Radio. Fascinated by what he heard, he found a hunger growing in him to know more about the Lord Jesus. However, back in the 1980s, he knew that it was far too dangerous to make any moves in that direction in his situation in China. Intellectuals like him have suffered much over the years for any 'deviation', and he did not dare to do more than listen secretly to the Christian radio programmes beamed in from abroad.

Then he was given an opportunity to spend a period of time in England to do some research. He made up his mind that he would seek the truth about God in that freer environment. However, his initial efforts proved futile. Unfortunately, and not necessarily typically, the UK churches near where he was staying seemed dull and uninteresting. Their content seemed almost unrelated to the Christianity that he had heard about on the radio programmes back in China. Sadly, he did not find the relationship with God that he was looking for. He therefore gave up looking in churches for the answer to his need. He resorted to watching television, hoping that he might find the answer there.

That could have been the sad end to this anecdote. One wonders how many students from overseas have come to the West with a genuine openness to Christianity, but have returned to their countries, sometimes after years, not having encountered the living Christ or any genuine Christians, and have remained disillusioned. Thankfully, that was not the case here. One day a Christian lady came into contact with Professor Zhou. She attended a social gathering, to which he also had been invited. Perhaps she was there to 'fish' for just such a prepared heart. After Zhou had shared his predicament, she invited him to attend a meeting in her church. God met with Professor Zhou in that church meeting in a powerful way – so much that was said there under the leading of the Holy Spirit seemed to be directly addressed to him. Thus at last he came to faith in the Lord Jesus, accepting His finished work on the cross and receiving Him as his personal Saviour.

During the rest of his time in England, Professor Zhou took every opportunity to study the Bible. He knew that once he returned to China, he would have little chance to do so, and that he must redeem the time in England. I do not think that he knew any Christians back in China. After he returned, he continued that lonely walk – hence the tears when we met and prayed together.

The lessons here are compelling. First, a spiritually hungry Chinese scholar of real quality came to a Western nation looking for Jesus Christ, and yet was unable to find Him in the first churches he visited. Of course that would not always be true. Yet the fact is that, by himself, this man could not find Jesus in a Western country, even though he was specifically looking for Him!

Then, one Christian lady, sensitive to the leading of the Holy Spirit, became like Philip with the Ethiopian government official in Acts 8:26–40. She cared, she listened to the Holy Spirit and she was thus able to lead a key person into an eternal and fruitful relationship with the Lord Jesus.

However, I am not recounting a story for its own sake, just to interest and bless you. The fact is that some of you who read these pages could be used of the Lord in just the same way. You could be involved personally with the Chinese, even if you do not have the time, training or finance to visit or work in China itself. This is a way of reaching 'the ends of the earth' without leaving your own country – and possibly without even moving from the comfort of your own home!

Since Deng Xiaoping initiated China's Open Door policy in 1978, China has sent tens of thousands of scholars and students to more than seventy countries for specialised training. After they have completed their training, this elite group of people are expected to return to China to help in the country's drive towards modernisation. Huge numbers of them are studying overseas – in the United States, Canada, Australia, New Zealand, Singapore and European countries such as Germany, France and Great Britain. There is a priceless opportunity for believers in these countries to reach out to them with the gospel.

Such Chinese scholars are divided into three main groups:

1. **Senior scholars**, usually professors or research scientists, sent by the government for one or two years' training or further research. They are not therefore normally working for a degree.

2. **Younger graduates** who normally have been involved in some form of government service or university teaching or research for at least two years. Often they go abroad to gain a prized doctorate from an overseas university.

3. **Scholars and students** of all ages who are privately financed, often by relatives in the West or other countries in Asia. Usually they are graduates who desire to gain an overseas qualification.

To understand their situation, we need to put ourselves in their shoes. We need to try to understand what they are like and what they feel about us.

First, they are in a strange and foreign country. Many of them are completely overwhelmed by what they see when they first travel overseas. They face loneliness, far away from family and friends – many are married and have left a spouse and child at home in China. Culture shock is a real problem. They may be confused by the foreign lifestyle and amazed at the amount of freedom people seem to have. They may well be totally shocked by the decadence in some areas while in foreign countries. Yet they are often very keen to understand Western culture and will be open to discussion about what they observe.

During the first few weeks, they are particularly in need of help. They need people to take time to show them around and explain how the system works, so that they can settle in as quickly as possible. They will not know where to buy cheap food, how to open a bank account or what they can do in their spare time. Christian students on university campuses have especially good opportunities for service here, particularly at the start of the academic year.

The Chinese have extremely high standards where education is concerned and they have a hard time understanding the lax approach many in the West take to their studies. They also have the expectations of their families and universities back home to live up to. It would be hard for us to compute how much pressure that brings to them, especially when, with inadequate fluency in the language to begin with, they find themselves struggling, perhaps for the first time ever, to turn in quality work. The drive to do well and to spend most of their time studying must be respected. They should not be put under too much pressure to take part in an endless round of social activities. However, offers of help with English (or other local languages), checking an essay perhaps, will seldom be spurned. There are many other kinds of help that can be offered, if done in a sensitive way.

A note of caution here: in the 'confused' moral environment of a modern university, it is unwise for a friendly Christian girl to try and befriend a lonely Chinese man, whose wife may be thousands of miles away – or vice versa. The crossed wires caused by such an attempt can often be very hard to untangle without pain and embarrassment, or worse, on both sides.

Second, these visitors are often very open to hospitality offered by local families. Christians in the host countries have a tremendous opportunity to introduce them to Christ, but I believe the key to that is first to offer them genuine friendship, love and hospitality. Many of them love children and miss their own. Remember that some may have left their one child while he or she is only a few years old, missing the unrepeatable chance to see them grow. They will be interested to find out what family life is like in a different culture, and so will enjoy being in a family or home setting. We have a large family and while we were living in England, Sunday lunch was always a bit of an 'event' for us. Every so often we would invite Chinese students in, sometimes but not always including a church service first. We never failed to sense their appreciation of being included for that brief time in our family life, so different from their own. They would also enjoy it when we took our children to visit them on campus, feeding the ducks, or some such thing, together with them.

Third, they may not be very well off financially. Government-sponsored students in particular may not have much spare cash. That presents us with great opportunities to serve them by taking them on days out to local scenic spots and museums. The Chinese will almost always bring you a small gift when they come to eat at your house. It may be some chocolates, a picture, a silk handkerchief or something similar. Their culture says they should do that. Express gratitude for it. Make sure, if you go to eat in the place where they are living, that you do the same. Nothing fancy – a tea towel or something of local interest is fine.

It is possible that they will be embarrassed if, having been invited to a home, they find that the entertainment is too extravagant. We need to be sensitive in this area. Remember too that they like different foods from us, and we must not be offended if they do not go into raptures over what we offer them. An American friend told me about a Chinese scholar who was invited to a Thanksgiving meal in the States. Replete with turkey and all the trimmings, he eventually returned to his lodgings. There he promptly cooked some rice to eat – he felt the need of something that to him was real food!

If you are especially honoured, after they get to know you, they may even offer to cook Chinese food for you. If you have opened your home to them at Christmas or Thanksgiving, you may find they will want to reciprocate to you at Chinese New Year – that to them is the traditional time for being together as families and cooking special food. Our family developed the taste for *jiaozi* (Chinese dumplings) after we invited a whole group of scholars in to cook traditional New Year food. It is still a family pastime for us to prepare *jiaozi* together, for guests or just for ourselves.

Fourth, they are not all the same. The Cultural Revolution stereotype must be put aside. They are as different in interests, political bias, spiritual hunger and food tastes as the people of our own country. Some are clearly hard-line party members. Some might even believe that China needs to revert to the Mao days – though that is a rarity now. Some are seeking answers and are open to Christianity. Others are not. Most are unused to the immoral and decadent atmosphere on Western campuses, though a few seem to get sucked into that.

Very often one or more is assigned to report to Embassy officials about the activities of their fellow scholars. Do not be surprised if they do not wish to talk to you on spiritual or other personal matters whilst in the presence of others. It may happen that, having been vocal before, they suddenly clam up. They may be nervous about someone else in the room. It is far better to invite one or two to your home, than a large group, as they will be more likely to talk freely in small numbers. Accept that there is much you do not understand and leave it at that. A love for them and the desire to make friends with them is essential, as is a sense of humility and a genuine wish to understand the background from which they have come.

Some tips for the nervous beginner!

There is one simple key – learn to listen to them. Remember that they are culturally quite different from many Westerners. They do not always say what they think, and even when they do, they may not be quick to say it. Give them space, accept them for who they are, and love them with the love of the Lord Jesus. This kind of friendship evangelism is a wonderful opportunity to demonstrate the love of God. It is also a chance to influence people who might well one day be important leaders after they have returned to China.

There are no invariable rules for witnessing in any situation, but there are one or two things that might help. A relationship of trust is all-important to the Chinese people. This will have to be established first through practical demonstrations of the love of God.

Chinese scholars will often accept invitations to Christian festivals or weddings, which will obviously be culturally interesting to them. But it is important to guard them against foolish questions of well-meaning people. They certainly should not be exposed to people who are likely to launch headlong into an attack on Communism! It is wise not to criticise the Communist Party or the present leadership of China. This could cause embarrassment and estrangement. You are unlikely to discover their political sentiments until you know them well as friends. Even Party members are unlikely to admit that that is what they are. The subject of politics is thus better given a wide berth.

A good working knowledge of the Bible is essential. It is also helpful to think through some of the questions that a scholar from a Marxist background might ask. The sort of questions posed might be: What is truth? Is it relative or absolute? Can the Party define truth and change it? Can yesterday's truth become today's lie? What is human nature? Can it be changed? Is it really possible to produce a society of selfless individuals? What value has the individual? Is Christianity a superstition to deceive people? Does Christianity have a solid historical background? Can you give evidence for the death and resurrection of Christ? Is not a belief in any form of miracles to be seen as mere superstition and therefore to be rejected in this modern scientific age?

It is always best to be as prepared as possible and to think through some of these issues. There are plenty of Christian books available to help you. The above questions may well be vital ones which will be of the utmost importance to the scholars who bring them up. But if your background is not an academic one, and you feel out of your depth in such discussions, just be honest and say so. You will not offend them if you are open and honest about that.

You should allow your friends to bring up the subject of religion themselves. It is always far better to answer their questions than to try and force the conversation down that road. There are bound to be opportunities to discuss Christianity when talking about life in the West. The matter will almost certainly arise naturally. There is no need to try and force the pace. Remember that it is the Holy Spirit's job to bring anyone to an awareness of their need for Christ. The most effective thing that we can do is love them and pray for them regularly, undergirding all we do with this powerful weapon.

When all is said and done – relax! You do not need to speak Chinese. They would not be in your country if they could not speak at least some of your language, although if you have a heavy local accent, you might find it necessary to slow down when you speak. You do not need to be an expert on Sino-European or Sino-American relations, or to be able to pronounce the name of any Chinese leader, or to be able to pick up ten peanuts in twenty seconds with chopsticks in your left hand!

Listen to what two Chinese students have to say about those who have demonstrated God's love to them:

▪ I was brought up to believe that Christians were evil foreigners, who brought opium to China. Now I know that isn't true. I want to get back to China and tell people that Christians are kind and loving people.

▪ You have given so much to us without expecting anything back. We have very little that we can give back

to you, but what we can do is go back to China and show
the love you have shown us to the people there.

There follow some initial steps which you can consider
taking, if you feel a desire to get involved with Chinese
people in your town.

- Begin to pray for them and also for a way to make
  contact with them.

- Find out if there is a Chinese church, or any other group
  in your vicinity, that is already involved in outreach to
  them. If so, they will be delighted if you approach them
  and offer your home for hospitality.

- Offer your services for English teaching. That may mean
  befriending a scholar's wife or child, who may not have
  adequate English to cope in the environment – and who
  may be desperately lonely and homesick as a result.

- Contact one or more of the China ministries that have
  concentrated on outreach to scholars. Find out from them
  what material is available for you to help in language
  teaching or in witnessing situations. There is much
  material on various themes that has been translated or
  prepared over the years. There are also lending libraries in
  some places. See addresses at the end of this chapter for a
  list of agencies you might approach as a starting point
  here. Some suggestions along these lines would include:
  - Use bilingual (English–Chinese) Bibles in language
    teaching.
  - Find and use material that has been specially written
    with Chinese scholars in mind. (OMF have produced
    some very good material.)
  - Some books are available on specific topics, translated
    from English, such as on child rearing for young
    families or concerning aspects of American or English
    culture.
  - Suggest using the Internet for much good material
    that is now available there. There is devotional mater-
    ial such as 'Voice of Hope' at www.voiceofhope.com
    for starters.

- Use lending libraries.
- *Overseas Campus* magazine in the States (*Hai Wai Xiao Yuan*) is very popular and good to recommend to Chinese friends.
- Chinese people love music. If your church or area has special musical presentations at Easter or Christmas, invite them to it as a cultural event.
- Tapes of music and sermons in Chinese are non-threatening because they do not require a response.

Two models of what can be done

The first model comes from the testimony of a long-time friend, who is a busy managing director of a growing company and an elder in a local church. He writes:

In 1994 I heard from a converted Mainland Chinese woman in her twenties that Chinese students who had come to England were really receptive to the gospel. Fed up with English people who were unresponsive, I decided to see what we could do to reach out to Chinese people with the love of God. With a group of like-minded people my wife and I set about putting on events that would appeal to Chinese from the Mainland or elsewhere. We tried a bit of language assistance, entertainment, Christian communication, social events, parties, trips out to the countryside – everything we could think of. Because at that time most of the Chinese in our city in the north of England were post-graduates with young families, trips and social events worked best for us. Better still, inviting people into our homes and hearts was the most effective way to cross the language and cultural barriers. Our programme of activities has varied over the years according to the number of Chinese in the area, and the age and interests of the group at any one time. Since we started in 1994, we have seen many Chinese students come and go. All will (we hope) have felt that we have liked them and befriended them without strings attached. Some have responded enough to want to come to church

services and Alpha (evangelistic) Courses, and some have
been converted and are now going on with God. Some
among our team are Chinese speakers, and that has been
helpful. However, no one has to be an expert. The fact
that Christians care enough about folks very far from home
in an alien culture makes a real impact. We value very
much the real friendships created with some, with whom
we still keep in touch, despite being separated by many
thousands of miles.

The second model comes from a church in Singapore. They
reach out to a different group, another sector of Chinese
'visitors' who also need to be reached with friendship and the
gospel. These are the 'blue collar' and manual workers who
are arriving, often in droves, in Singapore and other Asian
countries. They are needed for working on the building
projects that proliferate in that part of the world, since they
represent cheaper labour than is available nowadays from
elsewhere. This church, among others in Singapore, has
arranged outreaches to these men, which involve bussing
them in, providing them with a meal and fellowship, and
then offering them a lively and relevant time of worship
and Bible sharing. There are almost always believers (from
Henan often) amongst them. Often it is the love and care of
the Singaporean hosts that touches their hearts, for many are
away from wives and children.

When I spoke recently at one such Sunday evening meeting, I offered the men free tapes and literature that we
happened to have available in Mandarin. Since there were
over one hundred of them at the meeting, I pointed out that
we did not have enough for everyone. I declared that they
had to wait till the end of the meeting, and were not allowed
to slip out while I was speaking to get to the book table first. I
am not sure that I would do that again – my wife and a CCSM
colleague on the book table were in some danger of being
nearly crushed after the meeting by the flood of humanity
that rushed to get what books and tapes there were! But at
the very least it speaks of a real openness to spiritual things in
this sector of the Chinese workforce overseas.

It may not be so easy in other lands to reach out to these people. Yet, if we have the will, the Lord will show us the way. In the case of those who work in restaurants in the West, it could be by arranging simple Bible studies for them in their rest hour – which may be at 4.00 p.m., not a very convenient time for many of us. Or tutoring their children to help them with their English. Even the growing number of business people and entrepreneurs – some quite wealthy – who are a growing segment of Mainland Chinese in the West might welcome help of the same kind, to enable their children to cope with the enormous stress of schooling without sufficient language.

Whichever model we use, the most successful evangelists will probably be those who have been converted themselves since leaving China – if they can be found. They will carry the deepest burden and concern that others should have the same chance as they had to find the Lord. They may have to overcome their fear of being identified as Christians in public. They may be concerned that others will report back to China about their activities, and their faith will be noted on their records against them.

A girl who joined our staff in the early 1990s, and who has been working with us ever since, is a case in point. When she first came to England, there was a strongly active Chinese fellowship in her university. She was drawn to attend a special meeting where a choir from Taiwan was performing Christian music. She found Christ that night. Soon afterwards, she felt the Lord wanted her to give up her academic ambitions and work full-time for Him. Working on the scripts of the Derek Prince radio broadcasts, she grew by leaps and bounds in her faith, but would always make herself scarce whenever anyone else from Mainland China was around. She was plainly terrified of 'coming out of the closet' as a believer. One day the Lord spoke to her about her fear through a visiting speaker and she was mightily delivered from it. From then on, there was no looking back. She immediately became active in reaching out to scholars and their families on the campus and became one of the key workers in a local outreach to scholars. Even though she has now married and moved on to another land, she is still active in reaching out to her fellow-Chinese.

All you need to know is a secret that I have discovered over the years: the Chinese are (with, of course, some notable exceptions) some of the most honourable, excellent and quality people on the face of the earth. The privilege will be yours – and the enjoyment as well. But then you might say that I am biased!

Part of the vision of AM/CCSM is to give **you** a vision to reach Chinese scholars at universities in your city and to show you a strategy for doing so. We have numerous materials available in Chinese to help you, particularly when students begin to ask questions about your faith. I would encourage you to write to us and let us know how we can help you reach the Chinese in your own backyard.

A sobering conclusion

I have presented this challenge of reaching out to Chinese scholars and students as an opportunity, but it is really more than that. I believe it is a divine imperative or obligation that we should reach out sensitively to the 'foreigner within our gates'. It is a sobering reality that since the period of colonialisation, many of the world's leaders have been trained and educated at some time in the West.[1] Some will have had at the very least a curiosity to find out about Christianity when they came, because of the false perception that Christianity is a Western religion. But few will have had the experience of Brother Zhou at the beginning of this chapter, of having a 'real' Christian reaching out in the nick of time and turning around a near-disaster to rescue them out of disillusionment. It is unfortunately sometimes the case that life-long hostility to Christianity and Christians has resulted from very bad experiences they had in the host country. These might range from severe racial discrimination towards them on the one hand, to their own disgust at the laxness of morality and disintegration of family values that they observe on the other. In the light of this, I believe we should ask ourselves whether we will not be held to account if we **fail** to reach out to these people the Lord has brought to our shores.

Hebrews 13:2 says:

> *Do not forget to entertain strangers, for by so doing some have unwittingly entertained angels.*

We have no idea who the visitors we are befriending might become in later years. After Christine and I returned from Taiwan in 1979, we began to reach out to some scholars on a university campus near our home in England. One of the young girls who came to our home a number of times that year later became famous as a writer about China. She even on one occasion came to an evangelistic home meeting at which I was the speaker. Unfortunately in her case other 'voices' in her environment spoke louder than ours, and she did not become a Christian. But it was a comfort to know that she did at least hear the gospel while she was with us, and one never knows when in the future a seed that was sown might spring to life!

Those we befriend and entertain in our homes may not be 'angels', but they may be China's future leaders, for all we know, be that in the political, cultural or educational sphere. And we have the opportunity at a significant time in their lives, when many are vulnerable and open, to share by word and deed about the truth of the gospel message. Who knows what an impact our simple acts of friendship might make!

The Chinese are also very loyal in friendship. A caring couple befriended some Malaysian and Singaporean Chinese in London many years ago. Years later, they were invited to preach and teach in their churches and fellowships in Asia. The seeds they had sown in simple friendship and love are still bearing much fruit. We may not see much scope for that right now, in still-Communist China, but we cannot tell what the future holds.

In Mark 14 we read the story of the woman (in John she is identified as Mary of Bethany) who anointed Jesus with expensive ointment. When some remonstrated with her about the 'waste', Jesus defended her with these words:

> *Let her alone . . . She has done a good work for Me . . . She has done what she could. She has come beforehand to anoint My body for burial. Assuredly I say to you, wherever this gospel is*

*preached in the whole world, what this woman has done will
also be told as a memorial to her.*   (Mark 14:6–9)

'She did what she could' – what a beautiful, powerful
statement! The woman in the story had no idea of the
significance of what she was doing. She was, in fact, the only
one who ever had a chance to anoint Jesus for His burial. By
the time the ladies in Mark 16:1 arrived to do so, they were
too late because He had already risen from the dead! But she
had no concept of that at the time. Nor did she have any
inkling that she would go down in history for doing it. She
had no ulterior motive in what she did: the only thing that
motivated her was love for her Lord, and, prompted by the
Holy Spirit, with no regard for her dignity, she lavished that
love upon Him.

That needs to be true of us as well. We have the opportunity to obtain the Lord's testimony that we too did what **we**
could. The Lord of the Harvest has seen to it that people from
all over the world have come to us. All we have to do is reach
out to them with genuine love and interest (and no ulterior
motive). The Holy Spirit will do the rest.

Some addresses to help with outreach to Chinese scholars and workers overseas

OMF International Headquarters, 2 Cluny Road, Singapore
259570

Chinese Overseas Christian Mission, 4 Earlsfield Road,
London SW18 3DW, England

Director for Ethnic Ministries, OMF International,
28 Charter Road, Altrincham, Cheshire WA15 9RL,
England

Overseas Campus Magazine, Campus Evangelical
Fellowship Inc., PO Box 638, Lomita, CA 90717–0638,
USA

Christian Communications Ltd, PO Box 95364,
Tsimshatsui, Hong Kong

China Ministries International, PO Box 366, Peitou 112,
Taipei, Taiwan

See also the AM/CCSM and DPM addresses given in Appendix 4.

Note

1. Two immediate examples that come to mind are Zhou Enlai and Deng Xiaoping, both of whom studied in France in the 1920s!

Chapter 9

Hide and Seek: the Minority Peoples of China

In the early 1980s a Western Christian cautiously entered the Jokhang Temple in Lhasa, Tibet. God had stirred his heart, giving him a burden for the Tibetans. He had responded by reading about them and praying for them. Now, finally, he had the opportunity to visit this kingdom on the roof of the world. He was aware of the sensitivity of sharing the gospel in Tibet, but he was also praying that God would give divine opportunities to share the word of life in a meaningful and personal way. Armed with a small handful of yellow Gospels of John, he cautiously entered the Tibetan Buddhist prayer hall. He studied the faces of the monks who were in earnest worship. In his heart he yearned that they would worship the true God. As he stood there, his attention was drawn to an elderly monk standing on his own at the far left corner of the room. Sensing the Lord's prompting, he went over to give the old man a Gospel of John. The response he received staggered him. 'I had a vision two years ago,' said the Tibetan Buddhist monk with tears in his eyes, 'in which a foreigner came and gave me a little golden book about the truth. I've been praying and watching each day. You are that man!'[1]

This true story is a cameo of the purpose of this chapter. It is a heartcry that we should embrace one of the most daunting and serious challenges that we face in our generation. It is that the minority peoples of the world, including those of China, should have the opportunity to hear the good news of the Lord Jesus Christ. If we take seriously the Word of God, we cannot accept anything less than that as the responsibility of our generation. It is my specific prayer for this chapter that it might be used in one way or another to change the lives of some of its readers. The vision is that the minority peoples of our world should have, at least once in their lifetime, the opportunity to hear the gospel in their own mother tongue.

In Acts 1:8 the Lord Jesus made two parting and definitive statements to His Church. The first was:

> '...*you shall receive power when the Holy Spirit has come upon you.*'

The second:

> '...*you shall be witnesses to Me in Jerusalem, and in all Judea and Samaria, and to the end of the earth.*'

If we refuse to go to the ends of the earth, we are in direct disobedience to our Lord. The Tibetans and the other minority peoples are the 'ends of the earth', the most unreached groups, of our generation, to whom we are commanded to go.

The example above in the Jokhang Temple, though it is thrilling, is only the first step. We might be tempted to feel that if God has taken such an initiative, then we ourselves do not need to be involved. The opposite is true. It should inspire us to reach out to this man and his people, knowing that they are on the Father's heart. Where He takes such initiatives, we should follow. For that man and more than four million other Tibetans to embrace the truth of the 'golden book', it will take far more than this one-off encounter. It will take strategy and spiritual warfare. But more than that, it will take Christians who are willing to forsake their 'comfort zones'. The heartcry of China's hidden peoples is that there should be such dedicated Christians, soldiers of the cross, who will go and live long-term amongst them. It will involve costly battles to see such people won to Christ. Moreover, it requires the will and commitment of whole churches, not just of passionate individuals.

In order to look at this issue, we need to face the Scriptures honestly. In particular, we need to acknowledge the fact that it is God's plan to save men and women from every tribe and people upon the face of the earth. John in the book of Revelation saw this as a clear reality. Revelation 5:8–10 declares:

> *Now when He had taken the scroll, the four living creatures and the twenty-four elders fell down before the Lamb, each having a harp, and golden bowls full of incense, which are the prayers of the saints. And they sang a new song, saying: 'You are worthy to take the scroll, and to open its seals; for You were slain, and have redeemed us to God by Your blood out of every tribe and tongue and people and nation, and have made us kings and priests to our God; and we shall reign on the earth.'*

It is possible to approach that scripture in at least two different ways. We can rightly affirm that the Lord loves us and has saved us, and that we shall live and rejoice and reign with Him. We are blessed indeed. On the other hand, He makes it clear that we will not be alone in that privileged position. It is easy to miss the statement that is at the heart of that divine revelation, but we must not do so. The key statement is that there will be people there with us 'out of every tribe and tongue and people and nation'.

Some might respond by saying: 'That is fine as far as China is concerned. We know, and this book has confirmed, that God is doing a mighty work in China.' Earlier in the book you read the statement that perhaps 20,000 a day are being saved in China – so that Wembley Stadium or the Super Bowl would be filled every four or five days. You might want to argue then that China will be well represented in heaven.

No, it will not. At least not fully so. When the Lord in His Word says 'out of every tribe and tongue and people and nation', He does not mean 'China', as we see it. The 20,000 a day are largely drawn from the Han Chinese, who comprise about 91.9 per cent of the population of China. Near enough, you say. No, because the Chinese government officially recognises fifty-five national minorities who are not ethnically Chinese, though they are citizens of the People's Republic of China. They make up the 8.1 per cent that remains. They may be a small percentage compared with the more than one billion people of the majority Han Chinese, but that is not the issue. If there are to be some of each and every tribe and tongue and people and nation in China before the throne of the Lamb, then it is not a 92 per cent to 8 per cent equation, but a one to fifty-five people group equation. There may be numerically many more Han Chinese than there are of these smaller groups, but each of these groups must be represented. You may have heard of the Lisu, the Hui, the Uighur and the Naxi. But what of the She, the Bouyei, the Lhoba, the Derung, the Achang and the Oroqen? These are some of the unseen minorities of China, who have yet to be reached with the gospel, because they must fill in the Revelation chapter 5 gaps.

How we view China depends on how we understand the word 'nation'. We tend to think of a nation as a political entity or a country. However, this is not a biblical concept. A better understanding of the word 'nation' would come from the Greek word *ethnos*, which is more accurately translated as 'people group' or 'tribe'. When we think of the Chinese, the image that comes to mind is of those who speak the Chinese language, eat rice or noodles with chopsticks, cook sweet and sour pork, and who have an ancient and exotic script and a Great Wall that can be seen from the moon. But that understanding is true only of a few of the minority peoples of China. The Zhuang and the Manchu, for example, have become so assimilated over the centuries that to the Western eye they look indistinguishable from their Han counterparts. Only in language and religion can they be separated. But on the other hand, there are minority peoples in China who have little or nothing in common with the Han Chinese. The Turkish-descended Uighurs of Xinjiang, for example, are instantly recognisable by their defined Caucasian appearance, Turkish-related language, use of Arabic script and adherence to Islam.

Scripture clearly shows us that reaching every *ethnos* has always been God's deepest desire – a desire He fulfils primarily through His Church. With fifty-five minority groups other than the Han Chinese, China must then still be high on God's agenda for that strategic task.

Over the last few years mission experts, looking at the world's hidden people groups, have coined the expression 'the 10/40 Window' to encapsulate the concept that many of them live in a certain defined area of the world. The 10/40 Window is an imaginary rectangle extending from West Africa to East Asia from 10 degrees to 40 degrees north of the equator. This area is home to almost half of the world's population and contains the core of the unreached people groups who together share our planet – 12,000 of them. Within this area live many of those who have been so far the most resistant to the gospel, in particular, the majority of the world's Muslims, Hindus and Buddhists. Included too is much of China's land mass and most of her minority groups.

A people group – in China or elsewhere – is considered 'unreached' if there is no viable indigenous Church within that group. An 'indigenous' Church is one that uses the language and culture of its own people. A 'viable' Church is one sufficiently developed to be able to evangelise without cross-cultural help. That is true only for a few of China's minority peoples.[2]

Although the minorities only account for just 8 per cent of China's population, their importance far outweighs their numbers. They are distributed over some 60 per cent of Chinese-controlled territory, mostly around the sensitive northern, western and southern borders. They supply most of China's livestock and have in their territories most of China's mineral resources. Their music, poetry and customs have greatly coloured national life. For example, Uighur music influenced much of the Tang dynasty's dance and drama and the Yi calendar led to the development of the ancient lunar calendar, used in China today.

China then, seen in this light, can be described as a rich mosaic structure of different people groups. In 1912 when the Qing dynasty was replaced by the new Republic under Sun Yat-Sen, the first flag used by the new state had five colours, representing the five main races of China: Han, Man (Manchu), Meng (Mongol), Hui and the Zang (Tibetans). It was a tacit admission by modern China that it is a multi-ethnic society.

That mosaic, because it represents so many diverse peoples, has presented a difficult problem to the Beijing authorities over the years. The general policy has been one of assimilation. Han Chinese culture, language and history have always been seen as prominent. Therefore under this policy all minority groups were expected to become like the Han Chinese politically and culturally. The Communists defined their goal as 'integration' by which the distinct ethnic characteristics that separate the Han and the non-Han Chinese were expected to disappear, leaving only the dominant Han culture. The Communists have thus emphasised 'nationality', or belonging to one nation. Regard for ethnicity – or the differences between the highly diverse people groups – clearly has not been a major factor in determining their policies.

Traditionally the Han have regarded the minority peoples as barbarians. Indeed, it was only with the formation of the People's Republic that the symbol for 'dog' – which was included in the characters for the minority names – was replaced with the symbol for 'man'. Perhaps this policy originally stemmed from the thoughts of Huang Di, whom the Han Chinese view as the founder of their race. He viewed his kingdom's mission to be that of civilising these 'barbarians', by bringing them closer to the Han culture. Only then could they enjoy the blessings bestowed by 'heaven' upon 'its chosen people', ruled over by him, their emperor, the 'Son of Heaven'.

However, most of the minority peoples of China have been unwilling over the years to embrace the 'one nation' vision, preferring to retain their ethnic uniqueness. Government policies which were intent on destroying this view, sometimes have unconsciously reinforced the ethnic differences. Han migrations and invasions over the centuries have pushed many of the minorities into the more isolated, rugged areas of China. That isolation has tended to promote, rather than reduce individual ethnicity.

Keeping the minorities under control has thus been a continuous problem for the Han Chinese. Where there is a concentration of members of one people group with strong religious beliefs, beliefs which may well foster thoughts of independence and minority separatism, the Chinese government has always been wary. They see this as a threat to the

stability of China. This is particularly true of the Uighurs and
the Tibetans. The government's response to this has
consisted of forced 'immigration' of the Han Chinese into
the minority areas, paralleled by the establishment of a
strong military presence. Tibet and Xinjiang are heavily
garrisoned by Chinese troops, partly to protect China's
borders and partly to prevent rebellion among the local
population (as happened in Tibet in 1959 and again in
1987). The minorities are restless when they see large
numbers of Han immigrants brought into their areas.

Whatever the government policies may be, the challenge
to the Christian Church is a very clear one. It is to base our
approach on nothing less than the Word of God. The
Scriptures reveal that God's purposes clearly include every
single different people group. The vision is clear – that there
should be gathered to Him for eternity men and women 'out
of every tribe and tongue and people and nation', including
the She, the Bouyei, the Lhoba, the Derung, the Achang and
the Oroqen.

In the light of that, each believer, each church, has to be
willing to ask the question: is God's priority in this matter my
priority?

The size of the task

It is not possible in a book of this nature to give an inclusive
coverage of the minority peoples of China. There is not
enough space. I can only focus briefly on two categories of
people groups – the Tibetans and the Islamic peoples. But for
further reading, I have included a reference section in
Appendix 1 at the end of the book. Suffice it to say that
anybody who studies the facts and figures about China's
minorities will reach a simple conclusion: very few have truly
been exposed to the gospel; and even amongst those who
have, very few have a viable Church to show for it.

In our generation, we may feel that we do not have what it
takes to do the job. But it seems that our forefathers in the
faith, who did manage to do extraordinary things for God in
these areas, were also only too aware of their own inadequa-
cies and weaknesses. However, they had the capacity to lay

hold of God to enable them to take the gospel into places others deemed impossible. Their courage to step out and fulfil the Great Commission must be an example for us to follow. They obeyed and therefore set the pace for their entire generation.

William Carey, the father of modern missions, laid the challenge before us. He said,

> God has charged us with this gospel. Is not the condition of our Lord still binding upon us? We cannot say that the command has been repealed nor can we say that there are no creatures (left) to be saved ... We must expect great things from God and we must attempt great things for God.

God is still looking for the men and women who will set the pace for this generation of reaching the fifty-five minority people groups of China. As you read this chapter, will you pray? It is a challenge for godly and prayerful men and women to hear the voice of the Lord saying, *'Whom shall I send? And who will go for us?'* (Isaiah 6:8). You cannot truly pray that unless you are willing to be a part of the answer to your own prayer. At the very least, that will involve ongoing prayer and support for those who do go.

Two examples: the Tibetan and the Islamic peoples of China

Two of the most challenging groups are the Tibetans and the Islamic peoples of China. We will look first at the Tibetans.

The Tibetans

The Tibetans live in what is now known as the Tibet Autonomous Region, and also in other provinces of China, such as Qinghai, Yunnan, Gansu, Sichuan, Shaanxi. The 1990 census listed a population statistic of 4,593,330 Tibetans. They make their living by agriculture, farming, and some light industry. The main Tibetan religion is Tibetan Buddhism (known also as Lamaism). Other religions include Islam, some Catholics, and several hundred Protestants. Ninety-six per cent of Tibetans have never heard the gospel or the Name of

Jesus. A small number have been evangelised but did not become Christians – less than 1 per cent thus adhere to any form of Christianity. The Tibetan Bible was completed in 1948; some printed material is also available. But much of that material is in classical 'book' Tibetan, which less than 5 per cent of Tibetans can read. The majority of the literate – only about 27 per cent of the population – read 'magazine' Tibetan not 'book' Tibetan. So far very little Christian literature has been produced in that script. Gospel recordings are available in Lhasa, Amdo, Kham and Spitti languages.

The Tibetans have been the centre of much media attention, because of the profile of the Dalai Lama and some Hollywood focus in the late 1990s. Most of that centres round the fact that, although China annexed Tibet in the 1950s, Tibetans feel they are not Chinese nor a part of China. It is possible to get lost in the political debate, and to forget the eternal issue – that they need to hear the gospel.

There has never been a major spiritual breakthrough for the gospel amongst the Tibetans. The largest Tibetan Protestant Christian fellowship known to exist anywhere in the world is situated in another part of China. According to reliable 'Three Self' sources, there are about 200 Tibetan Christians meeting in that area. However, they face fierce opposition from local Tibetan Communist officials and also from the local Buddhist lamas. There are unconfirmed reports that there are several other house churches in the Tibetan region, and possibly two or three other smaller groups, mostly planted by Chinese Christians. Christian witness by visiting tourists and Christian teachers and professionals has also had an impact. Most of the monasteries in Lhasa and some outlying villages have received Christian tracts. However, successful outreach resulting in life-changing conversions remains painstakingly slow.

Since October 1990, a daily thirty-minute Christian radio programme called *Gaweylon* (meaning 'Good News') has been broadcast into the Tibet plateau. An evangelistic video and several gospel audio cassettes are also available for distribution.

The sobering truth is, however, that after more than a century of missionary endeavour, Tibet still remains virtually untouched with less than one thousand known Tibetan believers worldwide.

The Islamic peoples of China

The Islamic peoples of China present an equally daunting task. China has a far higher number of Muslims (almost twenty million) than Saudi Arabia! Islam first reached China over one thousand years ago via the Silk Road and the southern sea routes. It came by traders, not by missionaries. Today Muslims form a significant part of the population of Xinjiang, Qinghai, Ningxia and Gansu provinces.

The main Islamic groups in China according to the 1990 census[3] are as follows:

Hui	8,600,000	North China, Yunnan
Uighur	7,200,000	Xinjiang
Kazak	1,100,000	Xinjiang
Kirgiz	142,000	Xinjiang
Salar	88,000	Qinghai/Gansu
Tajik	34,000	Xinjiang
Uzbek	15,000	Xinjiang

Most Muslim groups live in the huge region of Xinjiang province (seven times the size of the UK or twice the size of Texas) which is rich in oil and mineral deposits. Following the government policies outlined above, Han Chinese settlers are now set to outnumber the indigenous Muslim inhabitants in the region, and the area has become increasingly turbulent in recent years.

All Muslim minorities except the Hui have their own language. The Hui, who are the largest Muslim group, are scattered throughout north China and have communities centred around a mosque or Muslim restaurant in all major Chinese cities. They speak Mandarin and in many ways have assimilated with the Han Chinese. Many Hui have a different appearance from the Chinese, however, with high cheekbones and round eyes, and, unlike the Chinese, Hui men also seem to have no problem growing beards! The Hui are called the 'Hidden Chinese Muslims' because of that assimilation, and therefore differ sharply from the Uighurs, who are more separatist and hostile to the Han Chinese. Nearly 50 per cent of the Hui live in the four north-western provinces of Xinjiang, Ningxia, Gansu and Qinghai, the highest concentration being in Ningxia (1,524,448) and Gansu (1,094,354) provinces. The Hui are China's third largest 'national minority' after the Zhuang and the Manchus.

The Hui are also the most urbanised of all China's fifty-five minority peoples, with as many as 40 per cent living in urban areas. This may be the main reason for their relatively slow population increase, as birth-control policies are more strictly enforced in urban than in rural areas.

There are reckoned to be a total of only fifty Christians among the Hui and no Hui churches. Interestingly, Henan Province has almost one million Hui Muslims. Henan also has huge church growth – but only amongst the Han Chinese. There are up to ten million Han Christians in a provincial population of over one hundred million. Astonishingly, this does not seem to be reflected in any impact at all being made amongst the large number of Hui people living in their midst. It is a very powerful statement of the need for specific and cross-cultural outreach to the minorities of China. It will not happen by osmosis. They need servants of the gospel, from inside and outside of China, set aside to reach them.

The task ahead [4]

What will it take to reach these peoples, to see them represented in the throng of Revelation 5? Modern mission leaders have defined three types of evangelism – E1, E2, and E3. Understanding these helps us to see where the problem lies and what needs to be done to rectify it.

E1 evangelism is where we evangelise our own neighbour, our own people group. No language or cultural learning is needed. Therefore, there are no real barriers to cross – of language, culture, lifestyle, etc. We may call this 'near neighbour evangelism'. For example, a fifth generation white New Zealander reaching out to a fellow Kiwi with the same background, or a Han Chinese believer in Henan reaching out to another Han Chinese non-believing neighbour would be E1 evangelism.

In the case of **E2** and **E3** the evangelist must penetrate significant cultural barriers. It is more difficult because it requires the person to learn another culture and language (or at the very least, another dialect). An example of E2 evangelism would be a Han Chinese believer in China reaching a Hui Muslim. A Han Chinese believer reaching, for example, a Bedouin nomad in North Africa would be E3 evangelism. When we understand those differences, we see that reaching out to the minorities would be E2 or E3 evangelism for most Christians in the world today. It is important to see that, if they are to reach out beyond their own people group, this applies to the Han believers just as much as it does to overseas Christians. This cross-cultural E3 evangelism is the hardest task of all.

By this definition, **evangelism** is sharing the gospel with those from your own culture (E1), whereas **missions** is reaching out cross-culturally with the gospel (E2 or E3). E2 can take place within the same country, but not with the same people group. E3 implies going to a country that is not your own, to minister to a people group that has little, if any, resemblance to your own culture.

Most missionary work in our day targets the people groups that have already been reached (those that have a viable Church within their community). It is not E3 or pioneer work. It is reaching out **again** to a people where a missiological breakthrough has already been achieved. That is necessary work, for the breakthrough may only be on a small scale. But 'frontier' missions involves going cross-culturally and working in an unreached people group, with no viable Church amongst them. Those are groups where no missiological breakthrough has yet been made.

With the minorities in China, as in many other places, the majority of the work which is still needed is frontier or pioneer outreach. Ideally, this would be evangelism of the E2 kind, with Han Chinese believers reaching out to the minorities. After all, they live in the same country and can communicate in a common language. Thus the move of God amongst the Han people is easier for the target group to understand, because of some shared ground between them. We may assume that is one reason why God is working powerfully in China today. He does not give His blessing simply for one people group alone. His intent is that the people group who are receiving His blessing (the Han in China) should choose to share that blessing with the surrounding people groups (the Hui, the Tibetans and so on). However, we can also see that because of the complexities of history and the perceived ongoing oppression by the Chinese against the minorities, E2 evangelism will be challenging and difficult in this kind of situation.

If these people are to be reached, there will also have to be E3 evangelism. That means that Christians outside of China must be willing to forsake their security and their familiar worlds in order to travel across cultural barriers with the gospel. This is no more than the men and women missionaries of previous days were willing to do. It will require of our generation the same separate, distinct, pioneering efforts to create 'beach-heads' amongst these groups, so that we may see churches planted and grow. It will also take team efforts, with churches, mission agencies and individuals working together in harmony. The end vision is to see multiples of growing churches amongst the Hui, reaching in turn to the Uighurs, who then in turn reach the Kazaks and so on, until all the Muslim minority peoples have been reached. With God, this is possible!

A case study

E3 evangelism has been successfully employed under God in China in the past. A case study may help us both to understand the nature of the problem and also to know that it is possible to see God break through.

The Lisu people, a minority tribe now numbering about 575,000, are today estimated to have about 200,000 Christians or about 35 per cent of their population. In the light of today's challenge to embrace the 10/40 Window, it is worth studying some of the elements that caused the gospel to reach, and so impact, this minority people in China.

The first element is that of availability to God and

surrender to Him amongst the early workers. The first missionaries reached the Lisu in 1865. They travelled westward across China on horseback for six weeks from the ancient Chinese city of Kunming, crossing range after range of rugged, snow-capped mountains, the foothills of the mighty Himalayas. One slip could have plunged them thousands of feet to the valley floor below. For years they had heard reports about the Lisu tribe, but it took them weeks of treacherous riding, to become the first missionaries to bring the news of Jesus Christ to the then savage Lisu people.

The second element was the willingness to be on the wrong end of severe cross-cultural encounters. Those first missionaries on their first visit in 1865 were immediately surrounded by throngs of giggling and suspicious Lisu people, who had never seen a white person before. Walking through the busy town, they wondered how they could ever relate the message of salvation to these people whom God passionately loved, but who were so foreign to them.

Right there and then they had to witness a horrifying event – the open killing of a Lisu woman. She was first brutally bound with rope by her husband after he had caught her in adultery. The mob shouted its approval as the woman was then skinned alive by him personally with a razor-sharp knife. Her screams of agony remained with them for the rest of their lives. But their presence in no way inhibited the murder. The measure of the cultural gap is that the husband probably never even thought that he should hesitate to kill his wife in front of the newly arrived white people.[5]

The third element was practical application of different kinds of skills to open a way for the gospel. The Lisu people had their own language, but it was not a written one. The early missionaries had a strong burden that the Lisu should have the Scriptures in their own language, so they invented an easy to learn Lisu script.

The fourth element was the recognition in ministering to the minorities in China that they were engaged in a fierce spiritual battle. J.O. Fraser, perhaps the most significant of the missionaries amongst the Lisu, did not think that ignorance was the real reason why the Lisu were not becoming Christians in the early days. A few who had responded to the gospel in several different villages had turned back to their old practices. As the gospel penetrated, families would come down with illnesses. It was assumed that this was an attack from demons, displeased that the people were no longer sacrificing to them. Fraser himself felt vulnerable, particularly along the slippery trails, with bands of robbers, a variety of illnesses and even attacks by the wild Kachin tribesmen. He recognised that physical obstacles were but another manifestation that he was in 'enemy territory'. He had long, serious bouts of depression from which he was only delivered through prayer. In places where occult practices were performed by local pagan priests, the spiritual opposition was particularly intense. Nothing frightened the people more than the presence and control of evil spirits in their lives.

The intensity of this battle forced Fraser to devote himself to long periods of prayer and a renewed search of what the Bible taught on demonology. He reflected on how the ministry, death, and resurrection of Christ had made Satan a defeated foe. The war had been won; however guerrilla warfare was still being waged over the lives of the people, who for the first time were presented with the gospel of Christ. Because of the demonic oppression that the people suffered, Fraser was inflexible in his conviction and practice that no conversion was complete until it included a total sweeping away of all paraphernalia used in demonolatry, including the shelf on which the pagan objects were placed. The break with the old life must be thorough for where there was a turning back from their faith, the people would restore the customary objects used in demon worship.

Fraser often asked others to join him in united prayer until 'the power of the Name of Jesus' brought deliverance. He travelled much over difficult terrain but preferred to concentrate his efforts on certain areas, even though no fruit was immediately apparent. He wanted to pray and persevere until the 'walls of Jericho' fell down. Prayer was the main weapon to liberate the Lisu from their demonic bondage. He encouraged his mother and other praying friends from Britain to organise small prayer cells and join with him in reaching the Lisu through their prayers.

The fifth element is understanding that each people group requires a unique approach. During one of his prolonged periods of prayer Fraser saw that the Lisu came best to Christ by families, or even by many families, in what he and others called 'mass movements to Christ'. In today's terminology it would be called 'people movements'. The Lisu themselves were influenced by seeing this. Each day Fraser faithfully preached the gospel in the open air, in teashops, in Chinese inns and around the Lisu firesides. Increasingly he focused on the people who would be the bridges into families, especially the village elders. The clan system among the Lisu was strong and, unless the village elders approved, it was difficult for even the father of that home to destroy the family altar and cease the sacrifices integral to demon worship.

A sixth element is a united vision to work with others. This involves a kingdom of God mentality, not a 'personal empire' one. Fraser never saw the Lisu as his personal kingdom. He always recognised the contributions of the other groups working among the tribe, which included the English Methodists, the American Baptists, the Vandsburgher Mission, the Swedish Free Mission, the Pentecostal Missionary Union and the Assemblies of God.

A seventh element is a firm belief in the indigenous Church. Fraser believed that the Lisu churches from the beginning must be indigenous. That meant that the building of their grass-roofed chapels, financial support for their preachers and money for their literature must come from the people themselves. The only foreign financial help was for Bible schools and textbooks. Such an approach was not common in the 1920s to 1930s, for mission boards mostly assumed that people as poor as the Lisu could not support their own Christian activities. However, this method was successful among the Lisu, since there was no competing mission agency using a money-stimulated strategy that would undermine Fraser's principles. Those principles were practical. Fraser studied agriculture to help them improve their farming techniques and thus support themselves better. Helped by a British botanical expert, he was able to advise the

Lisu on the crops and flowers that would grow best in this section of Yunnan Province.

His policies worked. Despite facing many obstacles, Fraser reaped the first fruits of his labours in 1916 as hundreds of Lisu families turned to Christ. What had been small flames of faith in the mountains was now a roaring fire. It ultimately brought thousands into the kingdom of God.

The Lisu story is an outstanding example of E3 evangelism. It shows what can happen when men and women embrace a vision to see Revelation chapter 5 become a reality in the lives of others. It is also worth noticing in passing that the work amongst the Lisu is a good example of E2 evangelism, as the Lisu churches subsequently reached out to other neighbouring tribes.

But the truth is that Fraser and others of his generation have now passed on to their reward. They have served well, and they have gone to their rest. Who will take their place in this generation? The Lisu may be there before the throne of the Lamb, but so few Uighurs, Hui, and Tibetans – not to mention the She, the Bouyei, the Lhoba, the Derung, the Achang and the Oroqen!

Isabel Kuhn was also a missionary to the Lisu people. When the Communists forced the Kuhns to leave China, she knew that she would probably never again live amongst the people she loved. She told the Lisu church, 'In heaven the other saints will only see my back. I will always be leaning over heaven's rail looking down upon my beloved Lisu church!' The fruit of her labours remains to this day.

The challenge to our generation is to see our lives laid down as hers was, fired by that same vision of eternity, for the sake of the unreached peoples.

Notes

1. Account given in 'Tibet Focus', *Revival Christian Church*, August 1995.
2. See Appendix 1 for more information on China's minority groups.
3. Taken from 'Islam in China', OMF China Prayer Letter, March 1994.
4. Many of the insights here and elsewhere in this chapter are drawn from *The Condensed World Mission Book*, edited by Jonathan Lewis (1996).
5. This took place in 1865, but Isobel Kuhn relates a similar event in 1938 (see *Nests above the Abyss*, OMF, 1947, p. 11).

References

Covell, Ralph R., *The Liberating Gospel in China: The Christian Faith among China's Minority Peoples* (USA: Baker House, 1995).

Lewis, Jonathan, *The Condensed World Mission Book*, condensed from the 3-Volume Manual *World Missions: An Analysis of the World Christian Movement*, revised material has been prepared and printed by permission of the publisher (William Carey Library, 1996). Church Strengthening Ministry, Philippines.

Stearns, Bill and Amy, *Catch the Vision 2,000* (USA: Bethany House Publishers, 1991).

Winter, Ralph D. and Hawthorne, Steven C. (eds), *Perspectives On the World Christian Movement – A Reader*, Revised Edition (USA: William Carey Library).

Chapter 10

The Valley of Decision

The first section of this book, which you have now completed, has been designed to provide you with information about strategic ways of serving the Church in China. The next section gives an outline of the historical and political background that has shaped China and her Church. But at this point, between the two sections, I would like to run you through a short reality test. Bear with me. I think it will be helpful.

Matthew 28 is one of the classic world mission chapters in the Bible. Verses 18–20 contain what is called the Great Commission – the promises and commission given by Jesus that have inspired the Church over the years to reach out to the nations.

> Jesus came and spoke to them, saying, 'All authority has been given to Me in heaven and on earth. Go therefore and make disciples of all the nations, baptizing them in the Name of the Father and of the Son and of the Holy Spirit, teaching them to observe all things that I have commanded you; and lo, I am with you always, even to the end of the age.'
>
> (Matthew 28:18–20)

Many of the men and women that you have read about in previous pages were challenged and changed by these verses – Morrison, Hudson Taylor, Fraser, the Kuhns and many others. Indeed, the whole of this book is based on the premise that Jesus really meant what He said – that as churches and as individual Christians we should 'go' to the ends of the earth, believing that our prime responsibility is to reach the men and women of our generation with the gospel, and see as many as possible saved, baptised, taught the Scriptures and discipled.

Do we believe that? More than that, do we practise it? If we do not, we need to bear in mind that we are not in rebellion against just some minor command of the Lord Jesus: we are in rebellion against His final command to His Church.

It is a useful exercise to put the three verses we are considering into their wider context. There are three separate sections in this final chapter of Matthew's Gospel, of which the Great Commission is the third. The first two sections can be taken to represent two of the main reasons why the Church fails to obey the Lord Jesus in this matter of world mission. These first two sections can be seen as stops on our journey, stops that fall short of the final destination – the Great Commission. Everyone reading this page will fall into one of three categories – either stopping at one of the first two sections, or going all the way to the end of the chapter to the place of obedience.

Of course there is a fourth category – those who have not even reached the beginning of Matthew 28, either because they are not saved or because they are not effectively walking with the Lord. But I am assuming that such people will not have got this far in the book!

The problem with the first two stops is that they are only transit stops, not destinations. If we stop there, we miss a significant part of what God has for us. We need then to clarify very carefully, before the Lord, which of the three sections of the chapter most resembles our situation. Only at the end of Matthew 28 do we actually hear what Jesus wanted to say to His Church. If we fail to hear that, we risk finding ourselves in outright disobedience to the Lord Jesus.

Matthew 28:1–10 – The first stop: the joy stop

This first section of Matthew 28 outlines how, in the critical days after the death of Jesus, His disciples passed from defeat into great joy and blessing. The summary words are 'great joy' in verse 8.

The chapter begins with the two Marys on their way to 'bury' Jesus:

> *Now after the Sabbath, as the first day of the week began to dawn, Mary Magdalene and the other Mary came to see the tomb.*

They came to the tomb out of respect and love, yet in great sorrow and sadness. But they then came into a quite different place of great joy, as they discovered that Jesus was not dead. He had risen from the dead. Verse 8 tells us that:

> ... *they went out quickly from the tomb with fear and great joy, and ran to bring His disciples word.*

The Christian walk is full of such moments of 'joy' and 'blessing'. We serve a loving heavenly Father who delights to bless His children. It is that way when we first come to a fresh saving knowledge of Jesus. Or when we see others come to that place, for whom we have prayed and to whom we have witnessed. Just think of J.O. Fraser working and praying and fasting for ten years amongst the Lisu, with hardly a convert to show for it. And then suddenly several thousand of the Lisu turned to Christ. It must have been hard to say who was the happiest – Fraser or the Lisu!

There are times when the Lord answers prayer in a way that floods us with joy and amazement. Or, as we read the Bible, some new word from Him breaks into our life, changing and setting us free. Or maybe His Spirit comes upon us in a new and fresh way. The American evangelist D.L. Moody described how the Spirit of God came upon him with such a revelation of the love of God that he had to ask the Lord to stay His hand. He could not take any more. It was joy upon joy for him. Going forth from that encounter, he continued to preach the gospel. The difference was that many more came to faith in Christ through his ministry than ever had before.

The source of our 'great joy' could be any one of a variety of ways in which our loving heavenly Father meets us with blessings from on high. And as He blesses, so we are filled with joy, just like those women on that first Easter day. Tears are forgotten as they are washed away by the blessing that our Father has provided in His love.

The passage goes on to say more of the joy that comes from heaven. One blessing was not enough. After the encounter with the angels, the Lord met them again with a further blessing. In verses 9–10 it says:

> *He himself met them, saying, 'Rejoice!' So they came and held Him by the feet and worshipped Him. Then Jesus said to them, 'Do not be afraid. Go and tell My brethren to go to Galilee, and there they will see Me.'*

As though the first blessing were not enough, there was more to come. 'Rejoice', said Jesus, in case they had not had enough joy for one day! It is such a good picture of the extravagant love that the Father pours out again and again upon His children. That is the word that sums up this first stage: 'Rejoice'.

I fear that too many believers have got into the habit of just seeking blessing after blessing, and the joy that accompanies the blessings. They pursue blessing in North America and in Korea and Argentina and anywhere else they can find it. That is not wrong. It is only wrong if we see that as the final stop. If we decide to stay there, we make what was meant to be a transit stop, a place of refreshment for the journey, into a place of disobedience. It is never wrong to seek to be refreshed by the hand of God; it is only wrong to refuse to do anything else but seek such refreshing, to make it into a lifestyle instead of a life source with which to serve the destination, the Great Commission of verses 18–20.

Jesus did speak to them words of great blessing at this first stop, but it was not His final word, His all-important word. If we stop at verse 10, we will miss that.

All that I have shared with you about prayer for China, about the need for this generation to reach those fifty-five minority groups, about the need for teams of willing servants to go and work in China's orphanages or carry in the Bibles and books or to go and intercede and evangelise, all of that will be lost if you stop here.

You are a steward of what God has done in your life, and you will give answer, as a steward, to Him. Paul states this in 1 Corinthians 4:1–5. Verse 1 says:

> *Let a man so consider us, as servants of Christ and stewards of the mysteries of God.*

We are nothing more and nothing less than that. What we have, we have as stewards from the Lord. Every blessing is a test of stewardship. Moreover, Paul states, *'it is required in stewards that one be found faithful'* (v. 2).

The next and logical step is that God will judge our stewardship of what He has given us. Verse 4 makes that clear: *'But He who judges me is the Lord.'* Obviously Paul prepared himself for that. Every revelation that he had, every move of the blessing of God in his life, all these were seen in the light of the fact that he was a steward:

> *Therefore judge nothing before the time, until the Lord comes, who will both bring to light the hidden things of darkness and reveal the counsels of the hearts. Then each one's praise will come from God.* (1 Corinthians 4:5)

That brings an entirely different understanding of the dynamic of the blessing of God. Are you walking in that light, the steward's light, the light of the servant of the living God?

The greatest challenge of the 'joy' stop is this: if I stop at this point, I will know much joy and blessing, **but nobody else will**. I trust that you will press through from the place of blessing alone and seek to move on in Jesus. Of course He will visit you again and again with His joy, because in His presence there is the fullness of joy. I trust that you are not content to see that as the final destination, because then your orientation is to yourself only.

Matthew 28:11–15 – The second stop: the opposition stop

If you move on, you will almost inevitably come to the second stop, which is the opposition stop. As soon as they moved into blessing, as soon as they embraced the resurrection of Jesus and began to share it, opposition hit them. Indeed, while they were still on the way to communicate that blessing to others, opposition was already manifesting itself.

Joy and blessing, it seems, attract hostility and opposition as surely as night follows day.

> *Now while they were going, behold, some of the guard came into the city and reported to the chief priests all the things that had happened. When they had assembled with the elders and consulted together, they gave a large sum of money to the soldiers, saying, 'Tell them, "His disciples came at night and stole Him away while we slept." And if this comes to the governor's ears, we will appease him and make you secure.' So they took the money and did as they were instructed; and this saying is commonly reported among the Jews until this day.*
>
> (Matthew 28:11–15)

They were still on the road when the opposition came, and money was at the heart of it. Money changed hands to stop the news of the resurrection reaching a waiting world. That is still happening – sometimes through bribery and corruption, sometimes just in the choices that we make. Like Demas (2 Timothy 4:10), we forsake the cause of the gospel because we love this present world.

At the heart of it was religious intransigence born out of the traditions of men, not the Word of God (Matthew 28:15). Then there were corrupt secular authorities and the misuse of governmental power, springing from an absence of the fear of God. And of course there were lies – evil, wicked lies against the truth and the evidence of the facts; lies which gave birth to more lies and denials.

Very often today these kinds of factors work against the testimony of the Church and of Christians. Whatever the nature and the roots of that opposition, it is both frightening and deadly. It will on occasions inspire men and women to seek to kill those who preach this resurrection message. That was so for Peter and for Paul.

Part of the battle is to accept that opposition is a normal experience for Christians. If we accept with Paul that *'all who desire to live godly in Christ Jesus will suffer persecution'* (2 Timothy 3:12), we are freed from having to seek reasons for it. It is just a normal confirmation that we are walking in a way pleasing to the Father – and in a way most displeasing to the devil.

Earlier in the book I shared some thoughts from Selwyn Hughes. They are worth repeating:

> What else can we learn from Scripture about our heavenly Father? This: He will not keep us from trouble but He will keep us in it. When Christian leaders hold out the hope that becoming a Christian means freedom from trouble, they push converts towards disillusionment. Followers of Christ suffer as much as others, sometimes more so. Those who believe that being a Christian will insulate them from adversity may well find their faith collapsing when they are under stress. What Scripture teaches is this: God will not save us from hardship, but He will save us in it. **Lord, help me understand that the world is a battleground, not a playground.**[1]

That is such a helpful statement. Opposition and persecution are a normal stop on the way – a stop that may be visited many times on the Christian journey. If we see that, it will help us not to cease our journey at this point in dismay and discouragement. We will then accept that, although the pain is real, it is – if we press through – also temporary. The Father who raised Christ from the dead will also rescue us, His servants, each time we pass this opposition stop, so long as we trust in Him.

Selwyn Hughes, several years ago, gave some very helpful examples from the lives of two great men of God, John Wesley, the father of Methodism and a man who changed England in his day, and John Bunyan, the author of *Pilgrim's Progress*. Both men hit this opposition stop, battled deeply in it, but passed through to achieve great things for God. Because they did not give up at this stop, God blessed them richly in the Great Commission. Had they given up here, they would have missed their calling in God, and we would have been the poorer for it.

> One who knew more humiliation than most was John Wesley, the founder of Methodism. As a young man he was ordained into the Church of England, but after his heart was 'strangely warmed', his evangelistic fervour resulted in him becoming ostracised by many members

of the clergy and excluded from the pulpits of a large number of parish churches. He was then faced with the choice of either giving up preaching, or preaching in the marketplaces and fields. His biographers say that when confronted by this possibility he went through a torment of soul that is impossible to describe. To his ordered and reverent mind there was something vulgar about taking worship out into the open air. The idea offended him deeply, but he knew that this was the only course left to him. When a friend remonstrated with him and appealed to him not to take his ministry to the public places on the basis that he ought to have some respect for his good name, Wesley replied: 'When I gave my all to God I did not withhold my reputation.' He took to the open air, saying: 'I consented to be more vile.'[2]

John Wesley faced a point in his ministry when to obey the Lord and to preach in the open air seemed too costly. But he pressed on. It could be argued that it was this step, as much as any other factor, that enabled England to experience the revival that followed, with many people coming to a saving faith in Christ. Who knows what would have happened if he had not been willing to surrender his reputation and his good name? Who knows what will happen if each reader does not press on beyond this place of pain and tears, refusing to surrender to opposition and discouragement?

John Bunyan is another classic example of this principle:

Incarcerated for preaching the gospel, John Bunyan was told, 'Promise not to preach and you can leave prison today.' He stoutly replied: 'If you let me out today, I shall preach again tomorrow.' Bunyan's enemies never shook him; it was his friends who came closest to shaking him. Some of them said: 'Your concern about your conscience is very beautiful ... but what about your wife and children? Who has to care for them? And what, in particular, about your blind daughter, Mary?' The decision was not an easy one for John Bunyan to make. Some would argue that his family should have come first and preaching second – and they would have a point. But Bunyan was adamant; he believed that he was at a turning-point in history when to compromise on the importance of preaching would have had a deleterious effect on future generations. It was said by one of Bunyan's biographers that after a visit from a friend who tried to get him to put his family first, Bunyan felt in his cell the shadow of Giant Despair. He fell to his knees, praying that God would keep him faithful. God did keep him faithful, and threw in *Pilgrim's Progress* as well.[3]

What a stunning example Bunyan is of a man who refused, by the grace of God, to settle at this middle stop. As a result, God blessed him – and many, many through Him. Many in China today highly appreciate the book that God gave him, *Pilgrim's Progress*.

The example and the inspiration of the Chinese Christians themselves in this area are both challenging and moving. How many are there who have faced imprisonment, separation from loved ones, and much opposition? They have pressed on to the end. They are the bearers of the revival that has flooded China over these last years. They continued on beyond the opposition they faced to the end of the chapter, to verses 18–20.

How then do we react to opposition and discouragement? Do we stop here? Do we decide to back out of the full pursuit of Jesus and obedience to Him at this point? We may not leave the Lord, but may still fail in this way. Simply backing off from the call of God in our lives is enough to bring a significant degree of failure. The regrettable truth is that some Christians do back off at this point, feeling that the cost is too high. They probably do that because they have little understanding of spiritual warfare. Opposition is like a cloud – press through it and there is greater blessing the other side. After the death of Jesus comes His resurrection. After the sorrow of Friday comes the rejoicing of Sunday.

Matthew 28:16–20 – The final stop: the Great Commission

This is the final goal, toward which the whole matter has been leading. These words were not given to superheroes, for verse 17 makes it clear that the context was of doubt and even failure. They were given to those who pressed through, to be there when it mattered. The men and women who heard those words of Jesus were those who had stopped neither at the first stop nor at the second. They had made it to the end.

> *And Jesus came and spoke to them, saying, 'All authority has been given to Me in heaven and on earth. Go therefore and make disciples of all the nations, baptizing them in the Name of the Father and of the Son and of the Holy Spirit, teaching them to observe all things that I have commanded you; and lo, I am with you always, even to the end of the age.'*

In the pages you have read in Section A, I have outlined the different ways in which you can be involved in serving China and its Church. There follow specific and measurable steps that churches and individual Christians can take in order to obey the Lord in this regard. They can be reduced into four clear categories. I believe that every one of us should be involved in at least one.

Category 1: Pray

I have devoted a whole chapter to this theme, so it is not necessary to say much more. Fraser saw revival amongst the Lisu, and Lamphia saw it in New York, because they set their faces to pray, along with others.

Apart from praying for China, pray for workers that you know who are involved in ministry into China. They really need your help and prayer. Acts 12 starts with Herod in full cry to destroy the church and Peter in prison. It finishes with Peter in full cry proclaiming the gospel, and Herod struck dead by the hand of God. How did that happen? The church prayed.

Category 2: Give to the work of missions

I mentioned earlier the church in Singapore that used their Saturday afternoons to collect recyclable materials, and then used the profits for mission. Teams and radio or literature ministries and orphanage work need such funds. See what you can do to redress a balance where it is the churches, not the missionary organisations, that have first call on the tithes and offerings. And by that I do not mean give less to your church, but give also for the work of world missions. The Lord loves to bless us when we are generous with what He entrusts to us!

Category 3: Go to the field

That is the heart of the Great Commission. You cannot obey Matthew 28:18–20 totally unless you – or someone with whom you are deeply involved in support – goes. It may be on a short-term team, or for a longer period. It may be to Shanghai or to a minority people. It may not be to China at all, but to some other place the Lord is calling you. But go! As I said earlier in the book, my prayer is that some reading this book would be called to the minority peoples of China. I pray too that many would be called to go to China in teams.

Category 4: Support, motivate and encourage

Many missionaries face great loneliness and isolation. Home churches have a sad tendency to forget them, and unconsciously ignore them. Why not seek to stand behind such people, writing to them and telephoning or e-mailing them, even visiting them, and encouraging others to do so. One frustration in our day is that often churches experiencing 'blessing' or revival do not see the need to use that move of God to encourage and bless their missionaries on the front line. We need to exhort our churches not to halt 'at the first stop', where we can selfishly squander the goodness of God on ourselves. Let us dare to be different in this matter.

Furthermore, you might find yourself being used as a motivator. If your heart is stirred for China, use that fire in your heart to go round churches in your area, to pulpits, prayer meetings and cell groups, to challenge Christians to **'pray, give and go'** for China's sake. (See p. 101 and addresses in Appendix 4 for more information on AM/CCSM's 'Reps Programme'.)

Where are you then? Bathing in the rejoicing of the first stop? Overwhelmed by the opposition of the second stop? Or determined by the grace of God to go all the way to the final stop, to obey the Great Commission?

The title of the biography of the great Chinese Christian Watchman Nee is *Against the Tide*. The title symbolises what it has cost individuals like him in China to follow Jesus. He was arrested in the 1950s and was, as far as I know, never released before he died. It could also be a suitable title for the biography of many other believers in China.

Against the Tide. That is not just true for China. Jesus had to live that way, and the Bible is full of such men and women. At one point Peter tried to persuade the Master to go with the tide. But by going with the tide, Jesus could not obey the Father. Paul also went against the tide. The leadership in Jerusalem rejected him or was suspicious of him, the churches sometimes turned against him, some of his co-workers left him. But he remained faithful and could, at the end of his life, say that he had not been disobedient to the heavenly vision (Acts 26:19). A vision from God immediately causes us to swim against the tide. It did for Paul; it will for us.

Surrendering to Matthew 28:18–20's call to mission is like that too. The man generally known to be the father of modern missions, William Carey, also swam against the tide. He had to face discouragement from family, from church and from friends.

As we look at the Christian life in this light, it becomes clear that obedience to God's will, to a greater or lesser extent, will always cause us to swim against the tide. However difficult that may be for the Church to embrace, it is none the less true. But how great is the reward for the faithful! J. Oswald Smith, that great man of world missions, wrote:

> I can think of no greater joy that could come to my heart in heaven than to have multitudes of African people, multitudes from the Indian subcontinent, multitudes of Asian people, stop me every now and again and say to me: 'We are in heaven because you challenged young people to go. You raised missionary money. You came to our country with the gospel. Now we want to thank you for your part in our salvation.' That, my friend, will be the greatest joy in heaven.

Smith adds:

> It will not happen if you have done all your Christian
> work in your own country, not unless you have invested
> something in the regions beyond.

Where does that leave me – and you?

Notes

1. Selwyn Hughes, *The Fatherhood of God*, my emphasis.
2. Taken from *Every Day With Jesus*, date and title unknown (CWR).
3. Taken from *Every Day With Jesus*, date and title unknown (CWR).

Section B

Chapter 11

The Ship in the Stormy Sea: China's Church and State

In the early 1980s, as a visitor to one of China's major cities, I was staying in a modest hotel. One evening it suddenly became apparent that many of the staff had left their posts. I found them in front of a TV screen. It was not a soap opera or a sports event that compelled their attention: it was the trial of some major political leaders in China, which was being given nightly prominence on TV. Political events in China are not peripheral to the ordinary citizens' lives, easily dismissed by the general populace as irrelevant. They are a central focus and a daily reality.

Almost two decades later, in June 1997, just days before Hong Kong returned to China, I sat in a meeting in a central Chinese city. Along with a number of others, I was attending, at the very direct insistence of the local authorities, a meeting that had been called by the Communist Party officials to celebrate the handover of Hong Kong. I was frankly taken aback by the intensity of some of the speakers, as they addressed the topic. I knew Hong Kong's return was important to China, and I believed it was a necessary historical step. But I was not quite prepared for such a volcanic expression of those emotions by at least one of the speakers.

We who live outside of China need to remind ourselves again and again that the few who hold political views intensely in China control the destinies of the multitudes of citizens who neither hold those views nor share their passion for them. Yet their lives will be shaped and affected as if by strong winds – for better or for worse, whether they want it or not. Like me, this majority will be obliged to attend the meetings and experience the events and the changes that follow, whatever their personal convictions might be. They will be silent participants in world-changing events, which they cannot ignore but are powerless to influence. The decisions of China's political leaders, and the events that they set in motion, affect every life in China to a greater or lesser extent – including and especially the Christian believers. Thus to understand Christianity in China, we must have at least a brief acquaintance with the historical and political events that have shaped modern China.

Although the history of Christianity in China dates from the seventh century, this summary will only deal with the nineteenth and twentieth centuries. As we begin a new millennium, we will look back over two hundred years of turmoil, upheaval, violence, uprisings, bloodshed and human suffering on an unimaginable scale. This history is the backdrop against which China's current dramas are being played out. As these events have unfolded, the Chinese Church has lived and progressed amongst them like a ship in a very stormy sea.

The nineteenth century

As trade routes into China were opened in the early years of the nineteenth century, the first Protestant missionaries set foot on Chinese soil. Among the pioneers was Robert Morrison (1782–1834), who was sent out by the London Missionary Society. His activities were confined to the Macao and Guangzhou districts in southern China but, by translating the Bible between 1807 and 1819, he laid a solid foundation for those who followed.

The so-called Opium War in the 1840s led to the colonisation of Hong Kong by the British and the opening up of five Treaty Ports to foreign trade and foreign residency. Twenty years later, a second treaty specifically permitted missionaries to own land, build churches and propagate Christianity throughout China. While these developments made China accessible to foreign missionaries, millions of Chinese lives were lost and destroyed through the use of the opium – perniciously introduced by the colonial powers of the 'civilised world'. While the seeds of the gospel could now be sown in China, other seeds were sown which would reap a bitter harvest in the troubled years to follow. The Chinese people had endured so much from foreign exploitation and interference that a fierce undercurrent of resentment and anger was generated. They often associated the gospel with imperialism and the introduction of the opium trade, which brought huge social destruction. Even today many Chinese around the world look back to these events, and see them as grounds enough for rejecting the gospel.

These two elements – foreign missionaries like Morrison on the one hand and the Opium Wars and the resulting exploitation on the other hand – represent one of the balances that we need to hold as we seek to understand the complexities of Church and State in China. There were events that represented fearful injustice inflicted on the Chinese by foreign powers. There were also many godly and sacrificial men and women who laid down their lives for the gospel of the Lord Jesus Christ. In the minds of many Chinese the two elements are merged together, and Christianity is viewed as an arm of imperialism. But we should not be confused by that into denying that the majority of the missionaries in those complex decades were genuine soldiers of the cross, who paid a great price for the sake of the gospel. In so doing, they laid the foundations upon which the massive church growth in China today has been built. The wheat and the tares grew up together.

The latter half of the nineteenth century saw sporadic rebellion against the Dynastic rulers. Between 1851 and 1864, the Qing Dynasty resisted the Taiping Rebellion. Wholesale slaughter accompanied the crushing of this movement, which was led by a man with pseudo-Christian aspirations of creating a 'heavenly kingdom' here on earth. The Taiping rebellion, though it took place one and a half centuries ago, still deeply influences the thinking of China's current Communist leaders. The explosive growth of the Christian Church in China over the last twenty years suggests to them the possibility of a modern recurrence of such a rebellion. Again, politics and history are dynamic forces in China, constantly asserting their power to shape and reshape the lives of the average citizen.

Despite these troubles, Protestant missionary activity was on the increase. J. Hudson Taylor (1832–1905), who founded the China Inland Mission in 1865, and his colleagues were breaking new ground in the interior provinces. By the end of the century, there were reckoned to be over 110,000 Protestants and almost half a million Roman Catholics in China. One result of this growing Christian influence was the development of schools, colleges and hospitals. A new and broader generation of educated Chinese people was emerging, drawn from a much wider base than the previous narrow band of intelligentsia. Though such institutions broadened the availability of higher education to many outside the privileged classes, yet they did not result in a significant turning to Christ amongst intellectuals.

Dr Sun Yatsen (1867–1925), the son of a Christian convert, was a product of the new education system. He practised as a doctor in Macao, but later turned his attention to politics and became involved in revolutionary agitation against the Qing Dynasty. He fled to the West in 1895, after being involved in a failed insurrection, but was destined to return in 1911 as the first President of the new Republic.

The nineteenth century ended with continuing unrest in China. Feelings of resentment and hatred against the colonial powers, which had long been simmering, were reaching boiling point.

1900 to 1919

The twentieth century dawned with the Empress Dowager Cixi encouraging the anti-foreign and anti-Christian Boxer uprising. In a tide of nationalistic fervour, about 32,000 Chinese Christians were slain along with 235 Protestant missionaries and Roman Catholic priests. However, the final outcome was that China suffered further humiliation, when allied forces invaded and took control. More land was lost to foreign control, as retribution was exacted on the Chinese people.

In the immediate aftermath of the Boxer rebellion, Christian missions continued to prosper. The gospel reached into the farthest corners of China, touching some of the ethnic minorities, as well as the majority Han Chinese people. In 1911, another revolt broke out against the Qing Dynasty but, unlike some previous insurrections, it was led by educated men who were riding high on a spirit of nationalism. The revolution was successful, and the Qing Dynasty came to an abrupt end. Dr Sun Yatsen returned from exile to lead the Kuomintang (Nationalist) Party. The new leaders of China were nearly all products of Christian schools.

Regrettably, Sun Yatsen soon had to give way to Yuan Shikai, the commander of what was then the only effective military force in China. It quickly became evident that Yuan wanted to be a dictator. Despite dominating the new parliament, the Kuomintang Party had little influence over the military. Civil war broke out in 1913 and, after Yuan's death in 1916, a power vacuum was left at national level.

Democratic government had failed to bring order to a China that was used to being ruled by those with the most guns. Events in Russia in 1917 cast a further shadow over China. Political thought turned towards the left. Leaders like Sun Yatsen began to look to Moscow and the Bolsheviks for an answer, rather than to the democratic systems of the old colonial powers.

At the same time, the First World War and the subsequent betrayal of China to Japan by the Western powers shook the faith of many intellectuals in the moral superiority of the West and thus of Christianity. China had been on the side of the Allies during the war. Once that ended, she naturally expected that the territory earlier held by Germany would be given back to her. When the Treaty of Versailles was concluded, however, this territory was left in the hands of the Japanese who had captured it from Germany during the war. The May 4 Movement of 1919 sprang out of a sense of outrage over this. Chinese intellectuals marched to the centre of Beijing, proclaiming the need for the Chinese government to stand up with strength and dignity against the unjust conditions of the Treaty of Versailles.

These events again did the cause of Christianity in China a great deal of harm, since, as mentioned above, the Church was inextricably linked with imperialism in the minds of many intellectuals and others. As a result, many of the intelligentsia turned to scientific humanism or Marxism. Left-wing students and thinkers founded an anti-Christian movement. It was partly because of this that the growing influence of Communism would be accompanied by the persecution of Chinese believers.

1920 to 1949

Hopes of a new society were kindled in the hearts of some in 1921, when the Chinese Communist Party was established in Shanghai with the assistance of the Communist International (Comintern). Mao Zedong was among the twelve founding members. Under the leadership of Li Dazhao and Chen Duxiu, the new Party set itself the goal of seizing power in China.

At first, the Communists and the Kuomintang worked together. Chiang Kaishek, who had emerged as military leader of the Republic after the death of Sun Yatsen, had visited Russia and appeared impressed by Soviet ideas. His successful military campaigns in the North brought some order to China in 1927. However, the emerging power struggle between the two parties was beginning to take the form of a violent conflict.

Several abortive attempts at armed insurgency by the Communist Party in different cities in 1927 resulted in a change of tactics. More emphasis was placed on peasant-based insurgency with the use of guerrilla warfare in southern central China. Mao Zedong was a keen advocate of this new strategy. During this period, he moved up the ranks of the Chinese Communist Party. His role lay in the development of those military ideas with specific application to the Chinese situation.

Against this backdrop of internal strife and guerrilla warfare within the nation, Christian missions suffered increasing persecution in the late 1920s. In the Communist inspired anti-foreign campaign of 1927, missionaries were withdrawn to the comparative safety of the coastal ports, and large numbers even returned to their homelands. But, as we saw in chapter 3, this was also the time when revival came to China. God was at work in these difficult events, preparing the Church for even darker days ahead.[1] The worst of the crisis was over by 1928, and in the 1930s there were times when some semblance of normality returned.

During the upheaval of this period, the Nationalists were in a position of strength because of their superiority in numbers. It became obvious to the Communists that, if they were to survive, they would have to increase their forces. They therefore made a strategic withdrawal to the mountains in the north-west of the country, a journey of 6,000 miles on foot through some of the most inhospitable terrain in China. The Long March, as it came to be known, took two years, 1934–5. The Communists suffered many casualties as a result of attacks by the Nationalist forces, but this amazing feat of endurance inspired many young people from the regions they passed through to join their ranks. Their goal of battling for a better life for the poor and downtrodden amongst their people also held great appeal for others. There can be no doubt that the impact of this epic achievement was deep and lasting. It is still held in high regard by the Chinese today.

In 1937, Japan attacked China, and for the duration of the Second World War, the Chinese people had yet more horrors to endure at the hands of a hostile foreign power. The Communist and Nationalist forces stood uneasily together to resist the occupation. The Japanese were eventually defeated by the Allies at the end of the War. When the Japanese surrendered in 1945, it was the Communist armies that found themselves strategically positioned to accept the surrender. At that key point in history, the Nationalist forces, led by Chiang Kaishek, were in West China, far away from these events.

Mao Zedong was by this time firmly established as leader of the Communists. They had gained more and more popular support, partly through stepping up their efforts to reorganise and reform local government, taxation and agrarian policy in the areas under their control. They had also earned much favour by the conduct of their troops, which by comparison with the Nationalists were generally well disciplined. This led to an unusually low incidence of plundering or civilian abuse in the rural communities through which they passed – perhaps because their targets anyway tended to be the landowners rather than the peasants. This discipline obviously made an impact on a largely peasant population which well knew what it was to be abused.

After the Japanese surrender, Mao met with Chiang Kaishek in Chongqing to negotiate China's future, but the failure of the talks led to a resumption of civil war. From 1946 until 1949, bitter warfare was waged. The armies clashed head on and millions of lives were lost. The smaller but better organised and disciplined Communist forces slowly gained the upper hand. The Nationalist forces were numerically superior, but their poor morale and other shortcomings eventually resulted in their defeat and exile from Mainland China.

On 1 October 1949, Chairman Mao, now the victorious leader over Japanese and Nationalist enemy alike, stood up on the Gate of Heavenly Peace (Tiananmen), overlooking the Square, where so much of China's history has been written. To a vast crowd representing a nation that largely welcomed him, he proclaimed victory over external oppressors of every kind and announced the founding of the People's Republic of China. To a Chinese people so abused, not the least by Western and other foreign powers, he expressed a sentiment that caused many Chinese hearts to leap for joy – China had stood up at last; the Chinese people had come of age. They were determined that they would never again be dominated, raped and plundered. Outsiders will never understand the dynamic of China's behaviour on the stage of world affairs unless they embrace the intensity of this emotion.

Meanwhile, the beleaguered Nationalist or Kuomintang forces took refuge on Taiwan, an island some ninety miles off the south-east coast of China, still under the leadership of Chiang Kaishek. The government in Taipei, the capital city, kept the title 'The Republic of China', as opposed to Beijing's 'People's Republic of China', making the point (the only one on which both sides agree!) that Taiwan is only a province of

China and that there should be only one government for the whole of China.[2]

Until the 1970s, with US backing, it was Taiwan that held the China seat in the United Nations. However, with Mainland China's increasing emergence in the post-1949 years, Beijing has taken over that UN place, as well as many other such international 'China' seats. Meanwhile, Taiwan's energies have been successfully focused on developing an economic base of remarkable proportions.

1949 to 1966: the first phase of Communism

A new day had dawned in the history of China, but Mao had no intention of letting the country settle down and rehabilitate in a peaceful manner after the horrors of the preceding years. Hatred towards their enemies, and the use of violence against them, were lessons that the Chinese Communists had learnt well from Marxism-Leninism. Two of Mao's much-used catch phrases reflect that: 'Political power grows out of the barrel of a gun', and 'Doing revolution is not like going to a dinner party'. Anti-Communists were rooted out and slaughtered in a series of reprisals. The landlord class were special targets for Mao's attention, and it is estimated that just under one million of these people lost their lives, with all their land being given to the peasants.

The next phase of Mao's strategy was the introduction of thought-reform. Chinese people of all ages had to undergo self-criticism sessions and join Marxism-Leninism study groups. Mao believed that by using such methods – purging people of their old way of thinking – he could create a new communist person. Such a person would show absolute loyalty to the Party and the cause of the revolution, would have a natural inclination to do good, and would be creative and unselfish. This model individual would be interested in the corporate rather than the individual good.

What a contrast exists there with the biblical truth that fallen humanity can only change through the redeeming work and power released to us by the Lord Jesus on the cross. No wonder many Christians in China faced a tough choice – to accept Mao's unrealistic humanist dogma and compromise their beliefs, or to hold to their biblical faith and thus be seen as unpatriotic and anti-Party.

Communism demands absolute loyalty from its people. To achieve this, however, it must control people's thoughts and motivations. An automatic conflict arises between Communism and Christianity, a conflict between atheism and theism. Atheism is basic to Communist dogma, which completely rules out any thought of the supernatural. It denies the deity of Christ and any suggestion of the salvation afforded to humankind by His death and resurrection. The possibility that humans are more than just physical beings – that they might have an eternal soul – is totally disregarded, as is life after death or future judgement. Communism denies the existence of an eternally valid moral law. This kind of thinking, human beings as matter only, without eternity in their soul, lies behind the ongoing low view of human life in China today.

Marx had had little time for religion. He saw it as a hindrance to the socialist revolution, something which had to be rooted out and destroyed. Lenin was even more forceful in his denunciations of anything to do with religion. It was his view that 'the roots of modern religion are deeply embedded in the social oppression of the working masses and in their apparently complete helplessness before the blind forces of capitalism. Fear created the gods. Every religious idea, every idea of a god, is an unspeakable abomination, a most repulsive infection.'

Thus, for the Communists, 're-education' and 're-moulding' became important tactics in handling religious people, including Christians. In fact, Christianity was singled out as a major target for vigorous attack in China, not just because it was considered to be anti-scientific, but also because it was identified with the imperialist exploitation of the country.

Paradoxically, Article 36 of the Chinese Constitution states that:

> Citizens of the People's Republic of China enjoy freedom of religious belief. No state organ, public organisation, or individual may compel citizens to believe in, or not to believe in any religion; nor may they discriminate

against citizens who believe in or do not believe in any religion. The state protects normal religious activities. No one can make use of religion to engage in activities that disrupt the public order, impair the health of citizens or interfere with the educational system of the state. Religious bodies and religious affairs are not to be subject to any foreign domination.

At first glance that article of the Constitution does in fact allow freedom of religion. A deeper understanding, however, reveals that much of the phraseology is open to interpretation by the authorities over their citizens. In Chinese Communist terms, those words were a temporary concession by the Party and by the State, permitting people either to believe or not to believe in their religion. The State thus offers to protect 'normal religious activities', but it also defines which activities are to be considered 'normal', in a way which is often hostile to Scripture. Communists believe religion will disappear from society at some point in time, through the joint forces of education and revolution. People will be freed from these archaic superstitions through social-ist revolution. Eventually religion will wither and die. They are committed to its death.

Once the Communists obtained power, all institutions were expected to obey the Party line. Many church buildings and other buildings associated with the work of the Church, such as schools and hospitals, were taken over by the authorities.

In 1950, a document was published entitled 'The Christian Manifesto', in which all missionaries were branded as imperialists. This being one of the ultimate accusations in Communist China, strong pressure was applied to Chinese Christians to require their missionary colleagues to withdraw from church work. By 1952, almost all of the missionaries had left China, sometimes under extreme duress. Some were murdered.

The new regime, under Mao, promised equality and social justice for all. Many young Christians began to feel that the Chinese Communist Party did perhaps have the answers to the problems facing China. As a result they gave up their faith, or considerably compromised it biblically, and became a part of the new order, sometimes in the process accepting the atheistic ideology of the government. Other Christians tried to divide their loyalties between the Church and the Party. They struggled to support a government that on the one hand seemed to promote equality and social justice and on the other believed in and promoted atheism.

A campaign was initiated by the authorities in the Church to root out all who were accused of infection by the 'imperialist poison'. In 1952 Watchman Nee, the leader of a major indigenous Christian work, was arrested. He was never released. In 1955 Wang Mingdao, a Beijing church leader who had refused to compromise with the State and stood against any political control of the Church, was also arrested. Although he had stood for indigenous church leadership, and practised it in his ministry, he was still accused of foreign contamination in a nationwide accusation programme. Wang was not released until 1980. Christians and non-Christians alike had to undergo daily indoctrination and re-education programmes.

In 1956, Mao launched a new initiative, known as the Hundred Flowers Movement, which was an invitation to all intellectuals to express freely their ideas and voice any criticisms they might have of government policy. The resultant deluge of criticism so shocked Party officials – who presumably had been expecting unstinting praise – that another wave of massive repression ensued, together with a further attack on intellectuals. Many were sent to remote parts of the country, some never to be seen again. Among them were many Christians. The policy of open criticism came to an abrupt end. Thereafter any criticism of the government came to be regarded as an act of treason.

Mao's plan was to turn China into an effective industrial-agricultural nation. In the late 1950s, the land that had been given to the peasants was taken back from them to establish communes. However, as a result of both severe flooding and drought, not to mention the disastrous policies of the Great Leap Forward (a failed attempt by Mao to increase productivity through unusual and eccentric methods in 1958–9), famine ensued. It is estimated that around thirty million Chinese peasants perished at this time.

All of this signalled a discouraging end to this first period of Communist rule. It had begun with high expectations and had clearly brought some economic and social benefit. However, the cost of that benefit was a catalogue of injustice and suffering, from which biblical Christians were by no means exempt.

These early years were very difficult ones for the Christian Church in China. Prior to Communism, in the first half of the twentieth century, there had been a steady increase in the number of Chinese citizens professing faith in Christ. There had therefore been every reason to be optimistic about the future of Christianity in China. Christians held positions of importance in educational and government institutions and were actively involved in social reforms and literacy campaigns. Christian missions had been playing an important part through their medical and educational facilities, as well as through their publishing programmes. By 1949, there had been a large number of universities, schools and hospitals operated by missions and churches.

Furthermore, as I said above, there had been, in God's wonderful economy, that widespread work of revival throughout China in the 1930s, which was described in chapter 3. This had not only acted as a 'cleansing gale of wind' amongst missionaries and Chinese alike but had also served to prepare the Church for the 'fiery trial' she was about to experience. Gone was much of the dependency on foreign support and leadership; gone too were many of the imported denominational differences. The Chinese Church was now beginning to take root and grow in genuinely Chinese soil. Chinese preachers and evangelists with powerful ministries had begun to emerge, men who became known in the West and all over Asia for their contribution to the cause of the gospel. These included John Sung, the 'Flaming Evangelist', through whom countless numbers were won to Christ, and Wang Mingdao, whose arrest has been mentioned above. Wang adhered strongly to the Scriptures and withstood heresies and false teaching. Watchman Nee is perhaps the best known outside of China. His in-depth, systematic study of the Bible has brought many Christians to a clearer understanding of the work of Christ in their lives. These and many others were taking responsibility for the growing Church in China, which was in some areas well down the road to becoming totally indigenous.

But the early years of Communism brought a sudden and hostile challenge to the very core of the Church's existence in China. As much as any in the land, Christians waited at the end of this first period of Communist rule to see what the future might bring.

1966 to 1976: the second phase of Communism

The failures at the end of the first period can be seen as the cause of the second period – the Cultural Revolution. Within the confines of Party walls, Mao came in for some very strong criticism. However, the architect of the Communist victory of 1949 was not to be deterred. He responded in 1966 with a plan to revive the revolutionary fervour of the Party.

The Cultural Revolution was part of Mao's theory of permanent revolution and class struggle, intended to give every new generation a chance to experience revolution for itself. It was his belief that cultural revolution should be repeated continually – if necessary, as often as every seven or eight years. Mao went directly to the youth of the nation, inciting teenagers to become Red Guards and take revolutionary action against the Party and State bureaucracy. All schools were closed, and Red Guards took to the road, opposing and destroying everything that they felt was in any way related to capitalism. The result was the almost complete breakdown of the institutions of government and State.

In political terms, the Cultural Revolution was supposed to rid the Party of 'old ideas, culture, customs and habits of the exploiting classes', in order to keep the flame of revolution alive. However, it quickly became a personality cult, with the Red Guards completely dedicated to Chairman Mao. The abiding image of China at that time is of young people zealously waving the *Thoughts of Chairman Mao*, the famous little red book, and reciting its contents from memory. One writer speaks of making her pilgrimage to Beijing that she might catch a glimpse of Chairman Mao. She longed to see his face. But she was sitting down as he passed by, and others, leaping to their feet, obscured her view. And so she missed her brief opportunity to see Mao's face. It was for her a moment of despair – as though her life's high point had passed her by.[3]

Following that initial explosion of revolutionary fervour, there came the second stage of the Cultural Revolution. Mao now admitted that the Red Guards had gone too far. They had become both a danger and an embarrassment to him. Millions of young people, intellectuals and Party and State workers from all levels were now sent to the countryside to 'learn from the peasants'. As a result of this vast influx of people into the rural areas, agriculture was placed under great strain. The 'peasants' despised the 'students', because they were a tremendous drain on the resources of the land, doing very little to add substantially to its productivity. The absurdity of that period is summed up by the experience of a slight Chinese lady, one of the first scholars to come to the West, whom we befriended in 1979. She described how, frail as she was, she had been forced to pull a plough in the paddy fields, 'while the oxen sunbathed'!

The educational system largely ceased to function until 1973. It did not begin really to recover until around 1977. As a result, a whole generation of young people was unable to complete its education. Revolutionary fervour was regarded as better than scholastic expertise. Scientific research largely stopped for a whole decade. Industry declined and urban residents suffered, as they were hit with one political campaign after another. Again, it is often impossible to speak with Chinese people who belong to that generation without picking up the bitterness they now feel about those events.

Christians were a prime target for the zealous Red Guards. Any church buildings which had not already been closed were ransacked and confiscated; Bibles and Christian literature were destroyed. Many Christians were publicly humiliated, assaulted physically and emotionally, and some even martyred for their faith. Leaders and church workers were forbidden to preach, and many were sent to labour camps, factories or farms. Some Christians were driven to such depths of despair that they committed suicide. For a time religion was declared totally illegal. Many Christians dared not even so much as greet one another when they met.

During this dark time, the faith and loyalty of many Christians to each other was put to the most extreme test. Some betrayed Christ and their fellow Christians. The fear of betrayal led to distrust even amongst the most godly believers. Despite the Red Guards' onslaught, however, the Church survived, and even spread to areas where previously there had been no testimony to Christ, often through the witness of believers exiled to remote areas of the countryside. Indeed, it was the testimony of some that had they not been in prison in those years, they would not have survived the ravages of the Cultural Revolution. God preserved the lives of many of His chosen vessels in prison, while using their testimony to reach the unreached!

Those Christians who escaped arrest devised ways of meeting, mostly in their homes in very small groups. Although the outward, public activities of the Church were severely impeded, the Holy Spirit was not. He continued to move in great power, with many people being saved, healed and delivered – including some of the Red Guards themselves, who could not help but be impressed by the lifestyle of the people they were persecuting.

In the nation as a whole in this second period, Mao's image had been dealt a further heavy blow, one from which he never fully recovered. When his Red Guards were either sent home or banished to work on communes in disgrace, they naturally felt they had been used and discarded, wasting the most important years of their youth. They were disillusioned, and mistrusted the Party and even the Communist cause itself. It had been a decade of terrible turmoil in China.

Throughout the early 1970s, Chinese Premier Zhou Enlai made strategic efforts to limit the damage caused by the Cultural Revolution. At a Party meeting in 1975, he proposed the 'Four Modernisations' of agriculture, industry, science and technology, and defence. The purpose of these modernisations was to bring China up to the standards of the West by the year 2000. These early events were the seedbed of progress that was to bloom in the next period under the leadership of Deng Xiaoping.

1976 to today: the third phase of Communism

Modern-day China presents a totally different picture from those dark days of the Cultural Revolution. The massive changes in the years leading up to the end of the millennium and the celebration of a half-century of Communist power seem almost to have eradicated the past. Chairman Mao would certainly not recognise today's China as the country he led for nearly thirty years. In the 1960s, during the Cultural Revolution, Beijing saw thousands of Red Guards marching through Tiananmen Square waving their 'little red books' in support of Chairman Mao. Today's China is more likely to see people demonstrating about a stock market scam. A decade ago, private cars were almost unknown. Today, China's roads are so crammed with vehicles that they are amongst the most dangerous in the world. Urban Chinese no longer consider colour TVs and refrigerators as the ultimate status symbols, so common have they become. Today their aim is to buy a private car and their own apartment. For the first time in many years, the increasing consumption of meat means that Chinese are beginning to worry about their weight. Everyone is looking for a way to follow the maxim of the chief architect of this new and different China, Deng Xiaoping, who said, 'to get rich is glorious'.

Deng came to power in 1977 soon after Mao's death, heralding the end of an era. The central core of radicals (the so-called Gang of Four), led by Mao's wife, Jiang Qing, had been arrested one month after Mao's departure. Deng quickly made the Four Modernisations his priority. Some desperate surgery was needed on China's ailing economy, which had seen very little progress for twenty years.

Agriculture was the first area to which Deng turned his attention. He was shrewd enough to realise that if people profit personally from the work they do, they are more likely to be motivated to greater productivity. Thus his reform of agriculture was centred around peasants' self-interest, rather than any revolutionary theories. An individual or household would be allocated a plot of land to work under contract to the State. The land still belonged to the State, but after those working the land had sold their allotted amount of produce to the State at set prices, any surplus could be sold off at a profit. The rural reforms proved to be amazingly successful. After twelve consecutive years of loss, in 1979 the State farms were able to announce an overall profit.

Urban reforms proved to be more of a challenge. The aim of these reforms was to replace the old system of direct control by the State with a system that combined both central planning and market forces. One effect of this was that China had to open up to the West, in whatever way was necessary to get Western technology and investment. The so-called 'socialist market economy' has led to thousands of individuals leaving their secure state jobs to set up their own private businesses. Western businesses have also set up joint ventures with Chinese firms, particularly in the 'special economic zones' of southern and eastern China.

Today, though Deng himself died in 1997, his policies are still the essential foundation on which the new China is being built. But there are three critical factors of underlying instability beneath this foundation that must always be kept in mind. They could yet bring Deng's new building tumbling down.

The first factor is that Deng's foundation represents the ascendancy of one wing of the Party, and therefore could be reversed. China's leadership over the last few decades has been troubled by competition between the rival wings of the Communist Party. The 'hard-liners' (of whom the Gang of Four were the chief example) have from the beginning believed that correct Marxist ideology and its communication to all within the State is the key to national prosperity. It has been said of them that they do not care whether the cat can catch mice or not, as long as it is pure red! Thus in the Cultural Revolution days they were content to allow economic, industrial and agricultural chaos and failure, intent only on pursuing a course of destroying all that was 'anti-patriotic' or 'counter-revolutionary'. That included any-one or anything the hard-liners regarded as incorrect in the light of their narrow and rigid views of Marxism – including of course Christians. For them economic chaos and industrial failure were an acceptable price to pay for the pursuit of ideological purity.

The 'moderates' or 'reformers' (the Dengists), on the other hand, hold a different philosophy, which is far more economically pragmatic. It can be summed up by the catch phrase: as long as the cat can catch mice, it does not matter what colour it is. Any cat that catches mice is a good cat! They saw that economic development had to come to China and that it had to come quickly.

Over the last two decades, the more pragmatic wing, especially under the leadership of Deng Xiaoping, has held the upper hand. Most China watchers feel that this is likely to continue. But now that Deng is dead, they differ in their views of the path that these leaders will take. No one can be certain what that path will be.

The second instability beneath the Dengist foundation is its inherent view of the relationship between political and economic change. In summary, economic change is seen as essential and imperative. But political change is to be resisted at all costs. On the surface the moderates seem to be agents of change. It is all too easy therefore to see the changes in China and imagine that the openness to the West means that the government is moving away from its Communist principles. In political terms, that is quite untrue.

This was seen very clearly in the government's readiness in June 1989 to massacre the students calling for democracy in Tiananmen Square. The Party is committed to maintaining its grip on power, and the State still exercises a great deal of control over the lives of individuals and institutions, including the Church.

In 1986, a decade into this period of reform and modernisation, Deng Xiaoping revealed his underlying manifesto. He proclaimed:

> Without leadership by the Communist Party and without socialism, there is no future for China. This truth has been demonstrated in the past, and it will be demonstrated again in the future ... We cannot do without

dictatorship. We must not only affirm the need for it, but exercise it when necessary. Of course, we must be cautious about resorting to dictatorial means and make as few arrests as possible.

Deng may have died and passed from the stage of history, but his thinking lives on in the minds of his current successors. After all, he hand-picked them. The rule of the Party is the ultimate, and other Tiananmens will happen if that rule is ultimately threatened – at least as long as this generation of leaders holds on to power.

China has rushed headlong into the modern era, whilst at the same time trying to hold to some form of Communist orthodoxy – at least in the continued, almost cynical, control of the Party over the people. The impression is often more of a tug-of-war than of a determined leap forward.

Christians in China have both benefited and suffered from this economic and ideological tug-of-war and from Deng's more pragmatic approach to Marxist ideology. When Deng came to power in the late 1970s, many believers were released from prison to take part in the Four Modernisations programme. Apart from the fact that they were needed to help in the programme, it was also necessary for China to present the appearance of religious freedom to the West. China realises that the human rights issue affects trade and diplomatic relations, and so she will do just enough on this issue to ensure that the West is placated. The central policy towards the West is relatively simple. It is to recognise that the West possesses much technology and investment potential that China needs, and therefore to do whatever is necessary to get those resources, without compromising the control of the Party.

Yet, at the same time, believers have to face the reality that, as the government fights to keep the country stable, they will often be in the firing line. Chinese President Jiang Zemin in 1999 again called for a crackdown on 'illegal religious activities' (which effectively means any Christian activity not under government control). The simple fact is that there are too many believers in China for an unstable and insecure government to handle. They are therefore seen as a potentially dangerous element – especially if they begin to work together in unity!

The third instability beneath Deng's foundation is the new social and economic factors that have been loosed by his economic policies. The leadership's control is weakened by the enormous social – or anti-social – forces that rend China today. They are forces that would have seemed impossible in the days of the Cultural Revolution just a few decades ago.

The eradication of the 'Iron Rice Bowl' is one such example. This represents the system that once offered guaranteed housing, employment, medical care and even pensions to millions of workers and their families – whether or not they produced much profit in the factories to justify their security. Whilst it represented excellent Marxist dogma, it did not sit well with an increasingly capitalist mindset. Economic reform demands the disestablishment of much of this system of security for the factory workers. But at the same time such a policy threatens the very stability of modern China. The vigorous pursuit of economic reforms may well lead to massive unemployment (to the tune of millions of workers) and also to the workers' loss of security.

Graft and corruption also haunt modern China, which, at the height of its Communist heyday, proclaimed that such things did not and could not exist. The pervasiveness of corruption, from the top to the bottom of the populace, is probably the most serious issue that the nation faces, and seems at times almost unstoppable. China in the mid to late 1990s executed more citizens per year than almost all other nations put together (at least as far as official figures record). Most of them lost their lives because they were caught embezzling or stealing, sometimes to the tune of millions of dollars. Some were Party officials.

These twin factors of corruption and social unrest through the threat of unemployment sometimes run together. Bosses filter company money into private accounts whilst workers go unpaid and become increasingly restless. Such factors should not lead us into wide generalisations about the Chinese people, many of whom are unusually industrious and able. But the growth rate of such crimes is serious enough to suggest that the Party views corruption and social unrest as major threats to its power.

Where will it all lead in the new century? China wants – and ought – to be recognised as one of the leading nations in the world. Yet her government is still facing the difficult choices about economic reforms that these three cracks in the foundation imply. The leadership has placed great emphasis on the need for stability. They have been seriously worried that unrest in any sector of society could lead to grave problems for them. Thus behind China's internal and international posturing of strength, there lies a deep concern about problems for which the new century will offer no easier quick fixes than the old one did. These problems demand replacement in the architects themselves and not just changes in their plans.

Few know which way China will head in the short term. Some argue that social instability, brought on by unemployment, corruption and the injustice that inevitably accompanies them, as well as other social factors in China today, could result in a turning back to the control and thought-form of the Cultural Revolution. It could mean that the hard-liners regain control. It is not likely; but neither is it impossible.

At the start of this chapter I mentioned an occasion when many of the hotel staff disappeared from view, only to be found watching the report of the trial of the Gang of Four on television. What impacted me at that time was the comment of a godly Chinese Christian, who said to me, as he observed the trial and the defeat of those who had caused so much suffering in China, 'God has heard and answered our prayers.' Even in the darkest days, God's people in China had called upon His Name, and He had rescued them – and the nation.

What does the new millennium hold? It is neither the dead (Mao Zedong and Deng Xiaoping) nor the living (Jiang Zemin and his successors) who will write the script for the future of the nation, calling into being the events which will ultimately direct the affairs of men and women in China.

It is a loving God in response to a praying and believing people.

Notes

1. Marie Monsen writes, 'In the last difficult years before the missionaries were all withdrawn from China, some Chinese leaders could say, "We have been blessed, cleansed, renewed by the Lord and we feel we can face whatever afflictions may come"', in *The Awakening* (English version, Overseas Missionary Fellowship, 1961).
2. The Nationalists were of course an invasion force when they arrived in Taiwan. The Kuomintang Party has always maintained the one-China view and cherished the hope of one day 'liberating' the Mainland. However, as time has elapsed and the old guard has died out, pragmatism has gained the upper hand in Taiwan. This has led to an increased momentum for the independence movement on the island. This unacceptable idea of a separate state of Taiwan has always provoked the strongest possible reaction from Beijing. Hence the periodic threats of missile attacks, etc. The Mainland Chinese government will not tolerate the notion of an Independent Taiwan.
3. See *Wild Swans* by Jung Chang (HarperCollins, 1993), pp. 425–7.

Chapter 12

The Three Self Patriotic Movement: China's Official Church

Since the Communist Revolution there have been, as we saw in the last chapter, competing factions within the Party. Both groups are of course committed to Communist dogma, but they do not entirely agree about how it should be applied to the different entities within the State. The 'hard-liners' stress the unwavering importance of correct Marxist ideology while the 'moderates' or 'reformers' usually maintain a more pragmatic approach.

Not surprisingly, the interplay of these two factions has directly influenced the life of the Church in China. The two sides have agreement regarding some religious policies, but take a different stand on others. Essentially, since the Communist Revolution there have been two different philosophical approaches within Chinese Marxism to the question of religion. The 'moderates' believe that education is sufficient to rid people of their religious beliefs and that religion will eventually be rejected by a socialist society. However, the 'hard-liners' want to obliterate religion as quickly as possible.

Except in the extreme period at the height of the Cultural Revolution, the vehicle through which both sides have worked to govern the Church in China is the Three Self Patriotic Movement (TSPM). This organisation was established by the Chinese Communist Party to liaise between the government and the Protestant churches. It is not a Church in itself, but is the only officially recognised **leadership** of China's Protestant Church. The equivalent for the Catholic Church is the Catholic Patriotic Association. The

Party sees the TSPM as 'the voice' of the Protestant Church in China, something which, as we have already seen, many Christians in China do not accept. It is thus impossible to understand the situation for Christians in China unless we have a clear understanding of the origins and the purposes of the TSPM. To do this, we will follow the three historical divisions of post-1949 China that were used in the previous chapter.

Pre-Revolutionary China and the 1950s

In the nineteenth century, a Presbyterian missionary by the name of John Nevius put forward the suggestion that the Asian Church should be self-governing (in its adminis-tration), self-supporting (in financial and other areas) and self-propagating (in evangelism and growth): hence, the term 'Three Self'. The concept was taken up by many churches, and well before the time of the Communist victory in 1949, there were already some genuine and successful models of indigenous Chinese churches, which were truly 'three-self' by John Nevius' definition above. Indeed, the Little Flock, led by Watchman Nee, would be one example of a whole move-ment which was founded on those principles. J.O. Fraser used these ideas very systematically in the work referred to amongst the Lisu in chapter 9 – many years before the Communists adopted the terminology.[1]

Against that background, in September 1949, Wu Yaozong appeared as the leader of a Protestant delegation to the Chinese People's Political Consultative Conference in Beijing. Many of China's Christians did not accept Wu as their representative. His own basis of faith – or lack of it – seemed at times to be derived more from socialist than biblical doctrine. He had doubts about the resurrection of the Lord Jesus from the dead and about miracles in general. Wu and those around him did not seem to feel that their denial of fundamental biblical truths was of any significance in their supposed and self-proclaimed leadership of the Chinese Church. China's largely evangelical Church was not quick to accept leadership from such a source, which bore the marks of a political, rather than a spiritual, agenda.

A year later, Wu and twenty other Protestant leaders met with Chinese Premier Zhou Enlai to produce the draft document, mentioned in the previous chapter, which was entitled 'The Christian Manifesto'. This document was basically a statement of loyalty by the Church in China to the Chinese Communist Party. The Manifesto was officially published in September 1950 and signed by 400,000 Christians.

In this document the Church's responsibility in Chinese society was designated. It included the following: Christian churches and organisations should give complete support to the 'Common Political Platform' and, under the leadership of the government, oppose imperialism, feudalism and bureaucratic capitalism. They should take part in the effort to build an independent, democratic, peaceable, unified, prosperous and powerful China. They should also do their utmost to ensure that people in churches everywhere recognised clearly the evils that had been wrought in China by imperialism. They should take effective measures to cultivate a patriotic and democratic spirit among their adherents, as well as a psychology of self-respect and self-reliance.

In 1951, over 150 leaders attended a national conference in Beijing, which was to deal with 'the disposal of the properties of American-subsidised missionary groups in China'. One result of the conference was the establishing of the 'Oppose America, Aid (North) Korea, Three Self Reform Movement of the Church of Christ in China' or the 'Three Self Reform Church'. An official slogan was adopted: 'Love Country, Love Church'. Wu Yaozong was elected leader.

The present-day Three Self Patriotic Movement is directly and inseparably linked to that beginning. In 1954, the National Christian Council held its first meeting, at which the emphasis shifted from 'reform' to 'patriotism', and the 'Three Self Patriotic Movement' (TSPM) was established, again with Wu Yaozong as its chairman. The Movement was and is responsible to the Religious Affairs Bureau, which is part of the government's United Front Work Department.

All Christians were expected to give their consent to the 'Christian Manifesto'. Notable among those who refused to do so were men like Watchman Nee and Wang Mingdao.

They were not in agreement with the Party's attempt to gain control over all the churches in China and they certainly wanted nothing to do with a movement that would be subject to Party policy. Furthermore, they maintained that they were already living out the 'Three-Self' principles in their lives and ministries.

In this lies the heart of the matter. A number of Chinese believers were at that time accused of being 'anti-patriotic', a charge that has continued to this day. That is not generally true. Most Christian believers love China and are not politically active against the government. Their opposition is to elements within the TSPM and its at times highly political agenda. In fact, if opposition to the TSPM is seen as being 'anti-patriotic', it immediately puts the TSPM into a political, not a spiritual, category.

By 1955, pastors and church workers who had refused to affiliate themselves with the TSPM came under vicious attack. The late Wang Mingdao, who had been born in 1900 during the Boxer rebellion, was a man with whom the Communists found it very difficult to find fault in terms of his spiritual walk or Christian service. He was pastor of an indigenous church (The Christian Tabernacle) in Beijing. Yet he was still charged with being anti-government and anti-Three Self. He was accused by the TSPM of being 'head of the counter-revolutionary foreign infiltration', and as a result spent a total of twenty-three years in prison, from 1955 until 1980. The TSPM endorsed the lengthy and unjust prison sentence imposed upon him.

The experience of Wang Mingdao was mirrored in countless other lives, and the complete story of the sacrifices of that multitude will only be revealed in eternity. Some TSPM leaders played a part in the imprisonment of many of these faithful servants of God, actively denouncing their evangelical brethren, or simply maintaining an evil silence and refusing to come to their defence.[2]

In 1957, a further purge took place. This time it was labelled the 'Anti-Rightist' campaign – a political campaign whose target was far broader than just the Church. But during this period, Christians who were opposed to the TSPM were branded as 'rightists' and suffered accordingly. Again, the political rather than spiritual nature of the TSPM leadership manifested itself clearly in these events.

By 1958, the TSPM had put out a decree forbidding all Christian meetings in private homes. At a TSPM conference held in Jiangsu Province, it was officially stated that 'all so-called churches, worship halls and family meetings which have been established without the permission of the government must be dissolved.'

In Shanghai, the TSPM resolved 'not to invite freelance evangelists to preach in our churches, and not to attend or preach in underground[3] services in homes.' In the same city, the number of churches had been reduced at that point from two hundred to under twenty. In Beijing, the number had been reduced from an original sixty-six places of worship to just four. Some of the pastors from these churches were sent to the countryside for re-education.

In many cities, only one Protestant church was allowed to remain open. The leaders of these few remaining churches were undoubtedly those who were prepared to compromise with the Communist Party. Through the TSPM, the Party gave strict instructions about the topics on which leaders could preach. Anything considered counter to the aims of the Party was forbidden.

Many Christians stopped attending the small number of churches that were left open, because they were TSPM-controlled and had frequently become centres for political indoctrination rather than for preaching the gospel. Some Chinese Christians began to meet in great secrecy in their homes. These hidden meetings grew into what came to be known as the house church movement, which will be considered further in the next chapter.

There was great danger for them in doing this, and many were arrested by the authorities. There is no doubt that some of the TSPM leadership was involved in the betrayal to the authorities of Christians who were meeting in this way. Any understanding of the realities of Church life in China today has to include this background as to why some believers in China feel that they are unable to trust or work with the TSPM to this very day.

The Cultural Revolution period: 1966–76

In 1966, the Cultural Revolution exploded onto the scene under the savage policies of the 'hard-liners'. It ushered in a new period of great hostility to the Church. Now it was not just the unregistered, non-TSPM groups that suffered. All churches were closed, including those controlled by the TSPM. At one time there was no freedom of religion whatsoever. Most pastors were arrested and imprisoned; some were even killed. Virtually all Christian literature was systematically hunted out and burnt or otherwise destroyed. One old Christian lady only kept her Bible by burying it in the soil of a flowerpot. Most Christians suffered greatly during the Cultural Revolution, but by God's mercy the Church not only survived, it grew!

The Cultural Revolution finally ended in 1976, yet in its wake there remained a legacy. The TSPM was still regarded with great caution by many, especially those who had suffered. They were suspicious of pastors who had denied their faith and even betrayed their fellow Christians during the accusation campaigns, but who re-emerged and continued to preach in the TSPM churches.

1976 to the present day

After 1976, with the death of Mao and the rise of Deng Xiaoping, the United Front Work Department was reinstated, and, under it, the Religious Affairs Bureau (RAB) was restored. Five religions were now officially recognised, including Roman Catholicism and Protestant Christianity, as well as Buddhism, Islam and Taoism. The TSPM once more, under the watchful eye of the RAB, took on the responsibility of implementing the government's religious policy in the Protestant churches.

By 1979 churches began to be reopened under the auspices of the TSPM. There was a concerted effort to draw people back to them, and the authorities even went so far as to try and persuade genuine evangelical pastors to return to TSPM pulpits, sometimes from the labour camps. Many believers flooded into the newly opened churches, rejoicing that once more they could worship openly and relatively freely in China's cities. When some of the Shanghai churches reopened in the late 1970s, for example, there were lines of people coming very early on Sunday mornings to get a seat.

In October 1980, a new organisation was formed called the China Christian Council (CCC). This new body was to concentrate on the religious affairs of the Church, while the TSPM would look after the political side. Bishop Ding was elected president of the CCC and chairman of the TSPM. The function of the TSPM was henceforth to make sure that all religious affairs were 'legitimate activities'.

The government's policy on religion was further clarified in March 1982 to all Party workers in Document 19 of the Chinese Communist Party's Central Committee, which was leaked to the outside world by some who felt that Christians outside China should know what was really happening. It is important to understand that Document 19 was not meant to be seen or read by most people. It was intended to be an in-house document for Party members only. Representing the official Party line, it is the hard face of Chinese Communist reality behind the mask of claimed religious liberty. It tells us what really is, and is not, to be allowed.

Document 19 and other similar documents permitted a limited amount of religious freedom, but many activities were forbidden for China's Christians, TSPM and house church alike. These included: Sunday schools; all evangelism among people under the age of eighteen; evangelism outside of specific church buildings registered with the TSPM; and all 'feudal superstitions', such as casting out demons and praying for healing. The official policy towards the house churches was made clear. They were not to be tolerated, but they could not be stamped out too quickly, because of their deep roots amongst the people. Considering the fact that the strength of the house churches is usually denied by official sources, it is remarkable that this statement is made in such a Party document. It provides evidence that the unofficial Church is alive and thriving in China today!

By this time, the TSPM had also established itself firmly at the provincial level. Steps were then taken to increase control further by establishing the supervision of Christians at county level. Attempts to set up TSPM and CCC organisations at this level were, however, sometimes resisted, particularly in areas where the house churches were strongest.

Christians gave clear and very understandable reasons why they were not willing to join the TSPM. One believer stated that the local TSPM pastor 'does not accept those who have been baptised elsewhere and will not allow them to attend the Lord's Supper. He also prohibits meetings in the home. Only worship once on Sunday is allowed, otherwise it is illegal and you are "unpatriotic". He won't allow children under eighteen years of age to even enter the church building, much less let evangelists visit believers in the countryside to have fellowship.'[4] Many other believers at that time had similar experiences and were resolutely opposed to their churches having anything to do with the TSPM, usually for completely biblical reasons. Substantial evidence points to the TSPM's often brutal co-operation with local security forces against believers, attempting thereby to remove any person and to stamp out any practice of which they did not approve. But that is by no means a uniform picture of the TSPM. Elsewhere there were and are godly men serving within it.

In early 1994, new national religious regulations were issued, entitled Documents 144 and 145. Their aim was to bring all religious activities, especially those of the unregistered churches, under state control. Document 144 clearly states that all places of religious activity must register with the government, which effectively means that all unregistered house churches are considered illegal. Another clause states that 'no one may use places of worship for activities to destroy national unity, ethnic unity and social stability, to damage public health or undermine the national education system.' Without a clear legal definition of those words, Christians fear that this allows the security forces to interpret them as they choose, in order to prohibit virtually any religious activity they dislike.

The significance of Document 144's insistence on registration of meeting places has become increasingly clear in the last few years. It was really the first official statement of an unofficial policy – that only churches openly registered and therefore under the control of the TSPM should be allowed to exist in China. There have been subsequent campaigns to enforce these regulations, sometimes with brutality. This is made the more sinister by the rise in corruption at all levels of society that has been described in the previous chapter. It is unfortunately true that some police authorities perceive Christians as 'soft targets', and use these regulations to impose fines on them (sometimes up to a year's wages), the money from which does not always appear to find its way into state coffers.

An evangelical perspective on the TSPM

In many TSPM churches there are good preachers, Bible studies and prayer meetings. There are many genuine Christians who attend, having little or no idea of the political or spiritual implications of belonging to such a church. There are also a good number of sound, Bible-believing pastors. The main issue is with the top leadership of the TSPM, which is strongly influenced by loyalty to the Party. In a local TSPM church, one of the leaders will normally be politically orientated, responsible for seeing that Party policy is adhered to and the rules kept.

If the organisation of the TSPM is viewed as a pyramid, the top part of the structure, the smallest but most visible part, contains the political element, which exercises control. Below them in the pyramid are the pastors, largely evangelical and desiring to serve God and His people. At the bottom, the widest and largest portion, are the laity, the generally evangelical stratum of the Church.

In 1988, a copy of a letter reached the West, written by an elderly pastor who had suffered greatly during the Cultural Revolution and had been imprisoned for many years. This leader may be said to represent the evangelical majority on the bottom two levels of the pyramid. After his release, he served the Lord in house churches, but when the TSPM set up a church in his city, he was invited to be a preacher there. He accepted the invitation because he saw the needs of the people. So, while sympathising with the house churches, he was regularly preaching in the TSPM church. This man, who was not extreme in his views, claimed that the leader-ship of the TSPM at national, provincial and municipal levels is, for the most part, comprised of either underground Party workers or former church workers who entered the Party after 1956.

He also claimed that the leader of the TSPM at that time, Bishop Ding Guangxun, joined the Party in the 1940s, when he was a theological student. He stated that his sources informed him that Ding held a senior position in the Party's religious structure. Though Ding has subsequently retired more to the background, such reports of a link between senior TSPM officials and the Party are quite common.

While evangelicals within the TSPM seem to have a certain amount of freedom in some areas of the country, overall the organisation is controlled by Party members. The founding 'vision' of the TSPM openly states that the aim of the organisation is to 'rally all Christians under the leadership of the Chinese Communist Party and the People's Govern-ment.'

With a nation as large as China, the implementation of TSPM policy will vary widely in different regions, from extremes of restriction to considerable openness. There is also a fairly wide spectrum of opinion among house church Christians about the organisation. Some are totally firm in their opposition to it; others are prepared to co-operate to some degree; and others register their meetings as govern-ment-approved 'meeting points'.

The arguments for and against involvement with the TSPM are many. Pastors who are against co-operation argue on the basis of 'Christ or Caesar'. Christ is the Lord of the Church and is, therefore, the only One who has final authority on matters that relate to the Church, and He has revealed His will in the Bible. In TSPM churches, the Communist Party has the final say on many issues. The TSPM's motto is 'Ai Guo Ai Jiao' ('Love your Country, Love your Religion' – in that order). If Christ is not the head of the body, argue these pastors, is the body beneath the head really following the Lord of the Church?

These Christians also argue that though the TSPM appears to be supportive of the Church, in fact it has sometimes acted, and does still act, in ways that contradict this. It has at times restricted as much as possible the development of the Church.

Furthermore, the government makes use of the TSPM to infiltrate and take control of the house churches. The TSPM offers help in the form of Bibles, hymnbooks and preachers, but the price is sometimes that the leadership of the house churches is effectively replaced by TSPM-approved personnel. Others point to the fact that lists of names gathered by the TSPM in the 1950s formed one resource for government attacks on Christians in subsequent campaigns.

But other leaders feel that a degree of co-operation is possible. They argue that there are many people, especially those who live in the cities, whose only chance ever to hear the gospel is in a TSPM church. The TSPM should not be blindly opposed. They argue that there are many godly TSPM pastors, and those who are not in that category would at least not oppose Christ publicly in the pulpit. The TSPM, they reason, at least provides legitimacy with the State for Christianity. It is a framework within which the Church can grow. The trellis (the TSPM) may be dead, but the vine has life.

Those of us from outside of China who seek to interface with her Church are not called to judge in this issue. But we are called to understand the history of the TSPM, and the process by which today's realities have been reached. A superficial view of recent church history and the TSPM's role in it may be convenient, but it is unlikely to be accurate. Documents must be honestly reviewed. Opinions of all Chinese believers need to be considered, especially those who have little opportunity to be heard. One such Christian wrote, 'This person is not the pastor of our choice. He was appointed by the Religious Affairs Bureau. We believers don't trust him at all. He persecutes Christians and has used church funds inappropriately. Quite simply, he is not a believer in our Lord Jesus Christ.' This was the courageous protest of a Christian from a TSPM church in Hunan province during the ordination of their new pastor. Such pastors are appointed by the authorities and are therefore not guaranteed to be believers. One TSPM leader admitted that there is a tendency for those who are politically acceptable, but spiritually unqualified, to end up in positions of leadership in the churches. If we fail to embrace such reports honestly, we are unlikely to understand the realities of Church life in China.

Visitors to China can be easily misled into thinking that all is well on the Christian scene in the country, when in fact real tensions exist. Their information is often funnelled through TSPM sources and they have no access to the house church. How can such visitors speak with any authority when they have no first-hand experience of the persecution which is very much a fact of life for believers in certain areas?

Whatever one may feel about the TSPM, many observers of the Chinese Christian scene would agree on one thing – it is not the only or the true voice of the Church in China. Its approach may have become more subtle and more sophisticated since the early days of Wu Yaozong, but the problems at the heart of its existence and original purpose remain unresolved. Therefore, over the years another Church, separate in both its foundations and in many of its values, has grown up and flourished, in the face of opposition. This 'other' Church will be the subject of the next chapter.

Notes

1. See pp. 173–7, 208 of Eileen Fraser Crossman's, *Mountain Rain* (OMF, 1982), for an amazing statement of Fraser's radical adherence to these principles whilst church planting amongst the Lisu in the 1920s.
2. My book *China: The Hidden Miracle* (Sovereign World, 1993) gives a fuller example of a Chinese Christian's experiences of persecution because of his faith during this period.
3. Refers to China's house churches. See chapter 13 for more insight here.
4. OMF China Prayer Letter.

Chapter 13

The House Church Movement: China's Unofficial Church

For fifty years of Marxist rule the Church in China has been wrestling with one central question – who is the head of the Church – Christ or 'Caesar' (the Communist Party)? This struggle affects almost every aspect of spiritual life. The battle centres around freedom to function in what I shall call 'the three alls':

- freedom to teach **all of the Bible** – including creation and the second coming;
- freedom to preach to **all the church** (including children under the age of 18);
- freedom to share the gospel **with all the people** (including those outside the doors of the church).

As we have seen in the previous chapter, the official Church sets firm limits on the freedom of believers in all three aspects. There are many true Christians who have been willing to live with that, for the sake of the benefit of being allowed to worship openly. But over the years many others have **not** been willing to accept the unbiblical limitations placed on them by the State. For many, the simplest answer to that problem has been to meet in small, unregistered units, a practice that Christians began to adopt in the late 1950s. In these units the Word of God can be preached, sometimes secretly, without political hindrance. There men and women can acknowledge Jesus as Lord and Saviour – under the leadership of those of like faith. Thus was born the movement in China that is generally known as the 'house church' movement. This is the 'unofficial'[1] or unregistered Church and it represents the vast majority of true believers in China.

In China the term 'house church' signifies a group of Christian believers, sometimes a very small unit, sometimes numbering hundreds or even thousands, who meet in a home or a farmhouse or some other informal building, or in the open air. The first thing, then, that we may safely say about the house churches is that they do not always meet in houses!

They meet in this unofficial way for a variety of reasons. The reason may be geographical in the sense that there may be no official churches in their area, so this is the only way that they can meet. Other groups meet in that way because of their spiritual convictions. They wish to have real fellowship and proper instruction in the Word of God, and do not believe that they can do so in the official churches. Yet another reason may be fear – they simply do not dare to be seen worshipping openly.

Whereas home meetings are a relatively new phenomenon in the West, they are nothing new for many Chinese Christians, especially those who live in rural areas. Even before the Communist victory in 1949, such meetings were not uncommon. However, since 1949 the China experience has proved to be the furnace in which a widespread house church movement has been forged. It is one of the most remarkable phenomena of the twentieth century.

There are some in the West who try to argue that there is no such movement in China. It would seem that they do not have access to materials available from inside China. For example, in 1998 a very significant document emerged. It came from house church leaders in China, and outlined why they are unwilling to join the TSPM or register their churches. As you read their comments, remember that these men risk their freedom to make the statements that are made here. They are not intellectuals living in ivory towers; they are pastors of the flock of Jesus Christ who might face imprisonment because of these words:

Why do we not register? Because the state ordinances on religion and the demands of the regulations for registration are contrary to the principles of Scripture. Because the state policy does not allow us to preach the gospel to those under the age of 18. Because state policy does not permit believers to pray for the sick, to heal them, and to exorcise demons out of them. Because state policy does not allow us to have communication with churches overseas, but the Bible teaches us that the church is universal.

Why do we not join the Three Self Patriotic Movement? **The heads of the two are different**: Three Self churches accept the state as their governing authority. House churches take Christ as their Head, and they organise and govern their churches according to the teachings of Scripture. **The way church workers are established is different**: Religious workers in the TSPM churches must first be approved by the Religious Affairs Bureau before assuming office ... house churches set apart their workers by the following qualifications: spiritual anointing, being equipped in the truth, possessing spiritual gifts, being approved by the church, and having spiritually qualified character. **The foundation of the two is different**: The Three Self churches are products of the Three Self reform movement which was initiated by the government; some of the initiators of the TSPM were not even Christians. House churches take the Bible as the foundation of their faith ... **The paths of the two are different**: The Three Self churches practice the unity of politics and the church; they follow the religious policy of the state, and they engage in political activities. House churches believe in the separation of the church from the state. They will obey the state when such obedience is in accordance with the Scriptures. When the two are in conflict with each other, they will 'obey God rather than man.' **The mission of the two is different**: The Three Self churches can preach the gospel, preach, and conduct pastoral ministry only within the designated places of religious activities.

House churches obey the Great Commission of preaching the gospel and planting churches.[2]

Aside from the outspoken nature of these comments, one point is clear. The issues that divide the TSPM leaders and the house church leaders are not peripheral. They are central to their understanding of Scripture.

In looking at the history of the house churches in China, it will help to refer again to the three periods of post-1949 Chinese history that have been used in the previous two chapters.

The first period: the late 1950s through to the mid-1960s

In the 1950s, as pressure from the Communists increased and the TSPM began to demand an essentially political allegiance from all Christians, many of those who refused to conform began quietly to meet in homes. In the countryside, where most of the churches were closed down, house meetings became the only way for believers to gather for worship, teaching and fellowship. In the cities too, as Party policy began to bite and the majority of churches were also closed, many Christians began to meet clandestinely, often in groups of just two or three. They gathered to pray, encourage one another and to break bread.

The habit of meeting in such a way was not foreign to the Chinese people. Chinese culture has always laid great emphasis on family life, and even though Communism has done much to try and destroy this, it has largely failed. It was natural for Christians to centre their spiritual lives in the home. Their house meetings were an extension of their everyday lives. This social factor would prove to be a great hidden blessing to the Church in China, and even more excitingly, the seedbed out of which would come growth on an explosive scale.

In the late 1950s the government quickly became aware of the widespread nature of home meetings and took active steps to suppress them. It pursued a relentless policy whereby private meetings – that is those not held in TSPM churches –

were forbidden. If more than two people were found praying together, they would be liable to be prosecuted on charges of counter-revolutionary activity and sent to prison. However, many Christians still met secretly in this way, risking arrest, prosecution and imprisonment.

It has already been made clear that much of the distrust of the TSPM felt by Christians in the house church movement originates in this period of the 1950s. The active participation by TSPM members (some of whom are still leaders in the TSPM today) in the arrests of some of those early house church members has left deep scars. It should not be seen, at least in some cases, as a lack of forgiveness by the house church believers. It is rather that they simply cannot accept that an apparent total lack of repentance for betrayal of their brethren is consistent with spiritual leadership of the Church in China.

The second period: the Cultural Revolution 1966–76

With the outbreak of the Cultural Revolution in 1966 came a fresh onslaught on the Church of Jesus Christ. Even the few remaining TSPM churches were closed, and institutional Christianity was completely eradicated from the life of China. As we have noted before, Bibles were burnt, and many believers were sent to prison or labour camps. House meetings continued, however, even though attending them had become more dangerous than ever before.

In some areas during this extremely difficult time, meetings of three or four believers for prayer and Scripture reading would take place at night. In spite of all the restrictions, some limited personal witness continued. As well as gathering in homes, Christians would also meet in parks, where they would pray with their eyes open in order not to attract unnecessary attention. They dared not preach or sing. It was a climate where citizens were encouraged to gain promotion by betraying each other in the rampant accusation campaigns. It was a step of faith indeed to meet in any way at all with other believers.

In a mining community, even after the Red Guards had confiscated all the Bibles and Christian literature they could find, a group of about one hundred believers continued to meet in one of the miners' dormitories for about four years. In order to avoid problems with the Red Guard Revolutionary Committee, they would sing as quietly as possible and also include a short time during each meeting for a study of the Thoughts of Chairman Mao. However, large gatherings of Christians such as this were the exception. The majority were very small, especially in the cities where surveillance was much tighter and the authorities were able to keep much closer control.

One report tells of meetings of a very exceptional nature. The situation was so dangerous that the meetings had to take place at a different time and a different place each week. It was impossible to do otherwise, or the meetings would have been discovered quickly and raided, and the believers arrested. However, there was another problem. Given the atmosphere of supervision by others and betrayal by infiltration, it was too risky to announce the time and venue of the future meetings. The only way in which a believer could get to a meeting was to pray and ask the Lord when and where the meeting was to take place. It is interesting to ponder how well we would fare under those circumstances!

The house churches in China grew out of practical necessity driven by persecution. Christians had nowhere else to go, particularly during the Cultural Revolution. Many denominational differences that existed before the Communist purges were soon forgotten in the common and overriding desire to have fellowship with other believers.

Many of the groups that met were without pastors and leaders, as they had been imprisoned. Yet the groups survived as they discovered new depths of fellowship with other believers. A unity was created that many of them had not known before the outbreak of persecution and, as a result, they discovered more of the true meaning of New Testament Christianity. The Body of Christ became more important than any building, as they experienced the presence of the Holy Spirit whenever two or three gathered together in the Name of Jesus.

During this time of severe trial and testing, the Church of Christ was purified. The half-hearted, uncommitted and false disciples were weeded out when persecution hit the Church. The Cultural Revolution was the crucible out of which was forged once more a refined and revived Church.

The third period: post-1976 China

In the mid-seventies, the situation eased a little, and in some areas Christians became bolder in their witness. It was, however, sometimes still hazardous to confess Christ too openly. Reports began to reach the West of quite large house churches in existence. In one area of the southern province of Fujian, there were reportedly two to three hundred young people meeting in unfurnished country buildings. From the same province came reports of a Christian community numbering around one thousand people, which had developed in the late sixties and early seventies. In 1974, five of its leaders had been arrested and paraded through the streets as punishment, but they were later released to continue their ministry.

After the death of Mao Zedong in 1976, the political climate relaxed further. Once Deng Xiaoping came to power in 1978 and the country was engaged in the early period of the Four Modernisations, the house churches enjoyed a period of relative peace. They no longer experienced the same kind of opposition and suppression as they had when Mao and the Gang of Four held sway. The Communist Party revived the United Front Work Department and encouraged non-communist sectors of society to play their part in the modernisation of the country.

As part of this United Front policy, certain religious activities were once again allowed. The Communist Party would say that religious freedom was granted once again. There is, however, a world of difference between what we outside of China would understand by religious freedom and the activities allowed under the United Front policy. This is the issue of 'a bird that is free in a cage' referred to in chapter 2.

As has already been said, the TSPM churches were allowed to open their doors again in the late 1970s. Many of those churches became packed to capacity. This alerted the authorities to the number of Christians that still existed in China in spite of years of persecution and 're-education'. Moreover, they were also quickly made aware of the huge numbers of people meeting in house churches – and the problems this created in terms of effective control and supervision of Christians. Hence their rather clumsy efforts yet again to bring together all the churches under the control of the TSPM and to make all meetings outside of the TSPM orbit illegal.

Between 1978 and 1980, most of the church leaders and workers who had been imprisoned previously as 'rightists' were freed. The authorities were certainly not thrilled by the evidence of the survival of Christianity in their country, and the reports of incredible growth in many areas were a serious setback to their Marxist orthodoxy. However, the political atmosphere at the time was such that excessive repression would have damaged their wooing of the West, which was so essential for the economic, scientific and educational planks of the Four Modernisations.

This was a peak time for the house churches. In some cities, huge meetings were held every night. They took full advantage of a situation where the local Party workers were treading very cautiously in their interpretation of the more moderate religious policy, sometimes even turning a blind eye to house church activities. Christians capitalised on the caution and confusion and became very bold, holding large meetings for worship, preaching and evangelism.

In some areas of China, the growth experienced by the house churches was nothing short of miraculous. In one county in Henan province, there were about four thousand believers before 1949. By 1982, there were eighty thousand. In another county, nearly 10 per cent of the population was estimated to be Christian in 1983. There were so many believers in Fangcheng county that it was reportedly dubbed a 'Jesus Nest' by local Party workers, one estimate putting the number of Christians as high as one third of the 826,000 inhabitants. In another area, there was a city where reports claimed 60 per cent of the population was Christian.

Some house church sources at that time estimated the total number of Christians in Henan province to be anything up

to five million people. In 1986 house church leaders spoke of
one independent grouping of house churches that had 2,500
churches linked together in fellowship. It was centred in
Henan, but covered five other provinces. The churches were
reported to be sending out evangelistic teams to neighbouring provinces – even as far as the borders of Tibet.

The history of the house church movement in China
represents one of the great church growth stories of all time
– and it continues to this day. Probably 80 per cent of China's
Christians worship in the house churches today. Some say
that 95 per cent of these believers have come to Christ since
1976. Through the faithfulness and courage of house church
Christians, who have risked much to bring the gospel to the
lost, whole villages have sometimes turned to Christ.

The house churches therefore represent the grass roots of
Christianity in China and are, in my opinion, the most
authentic voice of the Church of China. Over fifty million
believers in these churches have a different voice from that of
the TSPM spokespeople, one which we outside of China also
need to hear. What they say and what TSPM delegations to
the West say are sometimes totally different. The problem is
that it is logically very difficult for most of us to hear this very
contrasting voice of the house church leadership.

Whereas the TSPM leadership states that China's Christians have no need for Bibles, Christian literature, or gospel
radio, the leaders of the house churches say exactly the
opposite. They tell of the great hunger there is for the Word
of God, and the very real famine there is, in terms of the
availability of Bibles and Christian teaching materials. One
Bible shared between one hundred believers is not uncommon. Portions of Scripture are torn out of Bibles and
memorised or hand copied before being passed on. Sometimes these handwritten copies are circulated widely. It has
been known for believers to memorise huge chunks of
Scripture, even whole books. There are many who are willing
to travel hundreds of miles just to obtain Bibles and teaching
books for their churches from overseas sources. One young
farmer, only recently saved and with little Bible knowledge,
prepared a Bible teaching manual to help new believers. It
was estimated that this was used by at least 10,000 people.[3]

Is it any wonder that the house church leaders cry out for more Bibles and more teaching materials? They are experiencing such growth that they just cannot keep pace with the demand for teaching. Dare we on the outside, with our Bible and book mountains, ignore the pleas of our brothers and sisters? Will we allow ourselves to be deceived and lulled into apathy by the plausible sounding pronouncements of men whose first duty is not to Christ, but to the Communist State? Do we believe those who appear to be working to restrict the spread of the gospel and the meeting of believers, or those who share their faith by their lives and testimony, often at great personal cost?

Do we even take the trouble to hear their voice? I am constantly amazed at the way Christian leaders in the West fail to understand the nature of information control in a Marxist society. Many do not seem to realise that any official organisation, including the Church, will only be allowed to exist if it is firmly under State control. Its pronouncements and its official statements abroad will only be those that the Party permits. The functions of the TSPM come under such restrictions. Yes, there may be some legitimate attempts within those strictures to fight for freedom for believers. Indeed, some TSPM leaders genuinely feel that for them the only realistic course is to work within the 'system' and courageously negotiate for as much freedom for the Church as they can. But that does not mean that this well-intentioned segment can exercise any real control, nor that we should believe everything that is said from within TSPM circles.

We also need to understand that there are those who have endured much for their faith, and yet who are unable to communicate with us. Do we not know that they would love to share with us what God is doing in the house churches (and in many cases in the TSPM churches)? The practice of listening only to the voices of certain TSPM leaders in top leadership positions automatically silences the voices of house church leaders across China. Neither do we then hear the voices of the millions of believers that these 'hidden' leaders represent. We must be careful to guard against the gullible optimism of appearances, remembering that in China, few things are as straightforward as they appear.

It can well be truthfully argued that there is no one unified voice of the house churches in China, for they are a disparate and sometimes divided group. Yet a careful approach will persuade us that this actually is evidence for the **genuineness** of their voice, rather than the opposite. That is because their voices generally agree in what they share with us, constituting a chorus of harmony out of diversity!

When Billy Graham visited China in April 1988, he was allowed to visit the Premier at that time, Li Peng, and even to share the gospel with him. That is good, and we may see it as God's mercy to Li Peng. Yet Billy Graham was **not** allowed to meet Xu Yongze. Xu is a house church leader from central China, with a large number of churches in the movement that he leads. He came to Beijing specifically to meet with Billy Graham, to try and help the American evangelist to hear clearly that other voice – the voice of the house churches in China. Xu wanted to be sure that this godly American leader of such unusual spiritual stature really understood the situation in China from the point of view of the house churches. He was not sure that Graham would hear it from those he was going to see in China. But Xu Yongze never got to see Billy Graham. He was plucked off the streets by the security police and imprisoned for three years. It was easier for Graham to see the Premier of all China and to share the gospel with him, than to hear from a major spiritual leader in China about the house church situation there.

What a challenge that presents to evangelical leaders outside China! Conditions in China can alter very suddenly, depending upon the ever-changeable political agenda. If the Church in China should face another difficult period, the ongoing spiritual leadership of the house churches in China may in part depend upon our support. We must seek to understand better what is going on and to be wiser than we have been. There are days coming when the continued revival in the house churches in China may in part depend on that.

A decade and more later, this battle is still engaged. In 1998, in what was described as 'the most important document to come from unregistered churches in China in the last two decades' and a 'highly unusual and bold initiative', a group of house church leaders issued an appeal to the Chinese government to put an end to the persecution of Christians. The appeal was issued from Henan province, one of the centres of revival in China, and was drafted by twelve house church leaders from a number of different provinces. This was probably the first such public appeal from house church Christians to the Chinese government. It was also unusual in that it was jointly drafted by house church leaders from different areas. These leaders claimed to represent at least fifteen million Christians.

The unusual document urged a significant change in government policy:

> We call on the government to admit to God's great power ... We call on the legal authorities to release unconditionally all house church Christians presently serving in Labour Reform Camps ... All those who have been imprisoned for the sake of the Gospel should be released ... We call on the central leadership of the Chinese Communist Party to begin a dialogue with representatives of the house churches, to attempt to come to mutual understanding, to seek reconciliation, to decrease confrontation and to implement open-hearted interaction ... We call on the legal authorities to cease their attack on the Chinese house churches.
>
> History has proven that attacks on Christians who fervently preach the Gospel only bring harm to China and the government ... The Chinese house church is the channel through which God's blessings come to China. The persecution of God's children is a blockage to this channel of blessing. Support of the house church will certainly bring God's blessing. We hope the government will respond to this significant declaration of the house church.

In October 1998, just a few months after that letter was sent to the government, a few hundred house church leaders in different areas of China were arrested. It was an apparent response by the authorities to the letter. In spite of this, the house church leaders made another attempt to approach the authorities with a further letter.

Persecuted though they still may be, the house churches are yet the mainstream of Christianity in China today. They are genuinely seeking to follow the 'Three Self' principles set out by John Nevius. As the mainstream, they are more than deserving of our attention, our prayer and our assistance.

A decade ago, I had the privilege of meeting with brother Wang Mingdao in Shanghai. Though old and infirm in body and in the last years of his life, he was radiant in his love for the Lord. I asked him what he would like to share with his brothers and sisters in the West. His message was a simple one, which I have quoted frequently and will never forget. He said this:

> Jesus said to His disciples that they should not fear. Many stumble, but the commonest cause of stumbling is the fear of man. Jesus told us to believe, to trust in Him, not to fear ... In the 1960s, I was told that I was near to death, but here I am today. God has provided all that I have needed to serve Him.

Wang Mingdao has now gone to be with the Lord, but his testimony to the faithfulness of God still moves our hearts – especially when we know that it cost him twenty-three years in prison. The most fruitful years of his ministry were lost because of his betrayal by other official Christians. Dare we fail to hear what men like that are saying today?

On one trip to China, God spoke to me from Psalm 27:13–14 concerning Brother Wang and many, many other Christians in the house church movement in China:

> *I am still confident of this: I will see the goodness of the Lord in the land of the living. Wait for the Lord; be strong and take heart and wait for the Lord.*

These Christians have so little. They have faced so much. Yet, they have walked in faith in the goodness of God. They have proved His love again and again. There is an amazing stream of genuine spiritual life flowing amongst them. They are an addition to Hebrews 11 written before our eyes by the power of God.

May God help us to hear and respond to their heartcry.

Notes

1. The use of the word 'underground' to define these churches is deliberately rejected here, because that word implies constitutional illegality. China's constitution does actually allow freedom of religion.
2. Extracts from *China News And Church Report*, 21 December 1998 (emphasis mine).
3. Chapter 4 deals in more detail with the issue of Bibles and Christian literature in China, including a discussion of materials printed inside of China in recent years.

Chapter 14

A Final Question: What Will It Take?

Permit me to finish this book with a question: what will it then take to achieve this task of reaching China with the gospel and of serving her growing Church? For the answer to that question I would like to refer to an incident that happened about sixty years ago, a compelling story of the power of God breaking into the lives of men and women in western China. You may have gathered by now that the early pioneer missionaries to the Lisu people are among my 'heroes and heroines'. I have made several references to them throughout this book! The lives of such men and women who made up the missionary ranks of the past, and many like them in other parts of the world, constantly challenge me with their dedication, their selflessness and their effectiveness for the gospel. They can teach us so much. So we will let them have the last word.

John and Isobel Kuhn worked with J.O. Fraser amongst the minority peoples of south-west China. They had heard Fraser share at a meeting in North America, and in time had responded and travelled as missionaries to China. In the course of their work, they came to a village called Three Clans. The village was notorious for its fighting – perhaps not surprisingly, because there were rival clans within it, as its name suggests. It was, to be blunt, a fairly dark place. Isobel commented about it in these words:

> The lives of (these people) could never be freed by so feeble a thing as missionary witness and effort. They are

held under a tyranny of darkness so strong that only God is stronger! Only tremendous spiritual forces, working on the ground of the Atonement of Calvary, can bring light to such sightless eyes. That spiritual force is the prayer of many. The prayer of one or two missionaries or converts is not enough to break such bonds. We had reasoned, we had opened up the Word of God to the Three Clans, until their souls shivered with conviction, **but they still could not see the way out**, still they could not muster up the courage to break the custom of years.[1]

The stronghold over the lives of these men and women was a traditional one. The law of the clans was that, 'if any member of the clan gets into trouble, **whether he is guilty or not**, all the rest of his clan must back him up financially or otherwise. So if one man decided to steal a plot of farm land, the whole clan would have to help him steal it. If any man fail in this loyalty, when his time of legitimate trouble comes, he must face it alone – the clan will not help him.'

Like so many strongholds, the power of tradition couples with the bondage of fear – fear of being rejected, of being different or of being an outcast. Today, as then, these powers hold multitudes in our world in bondage, from simple tribal villagers to the most sophisticated of Generation X or Y young people in our cities.

The time for the Kuhns to leave the village was drawing near, but in their last few days there they sensed 'that the atmosphere of the village was softening, was changing.' But the last night of their stay quickly came, and still there was no tangible breakthrough. Isobel writes:

The night before we left to return home, my husband got an inspiration. We held a service in the chapel. John had decided to make an appeal for the abolishing of the law of the clan. John had prepared a set of paper arrows. On one set was written, 'I have no desire to practise the law of the clan.' On the other set was written, 'I desire to practise the law of love.' That last service together John very simply drew their attention to how Satan was binding them to sin by the law of the clan and though it would be costly to break away from it, followers of

Christ are bound to the law of Christ which is love – love toward **all** men, not just your own clan. 'Now I am going to ask all who henceforth will break free from the law of the clan and follow only the law of Christ to come forward, take the clan arrow, and burn it in the fire here. If you do this, I will give you a love arrow to keep always.'

Then he waited. There was no excitement, no play on emotion, but deliberately and slowly, one after another, leaders of the various clans came forward, took a clan arrow and burned it, giving at the time a short testimony, received a love arrow and returned to their seats. Some twenty did so – all the important leading fighters, **but one man**. (I always myself remember his name was 'Lamb', because the word, with the exception of tones, is the same as the Lisu for Lamb. The change of tones gives it another meaning of which I am ignorant, so I will just call him the Luda-Lamb for our convenience, though there never was a worse misnomer.)

Lamb sat silent, head down, looking up at John through shaggy eyebrows. My husband ignored him for the moment and turned to some famous old quarrellers. He publicly named the disputants and asked them to stand, seek each other's forgiveness and shake hands before us all. They did so. I myself had never been present at such a scene as God gave us to see that night. Two brothers who had not spoken civilly to one another for twenty-six years were among those reconciled.

Then John quietly sprang a surprise. 'Now, a certain man present has held a quarrel with the Oldest Brother' (of the two just mentioned) 'and I noticed that he did not burn a clan arrow. Luda-Lamb! Are you going to be the only man in the village to refuse the law of love?' But the Lamb sat silent and obstinate. He is one of the most powerful personalities in the community and was at the bottom of all the wormwood fighting ... Then, just as John was about to close the meeting, suddenly Lamb stood up and clearly and definitely made a public apology to his long-hated enemy, who likewise apologised, and they two shook hands.

> Luda-Lamb then came forward, plucked a clan arrow
> and burned it in the fire and took away an arrow of love.
> It was wonderful. Only God could have done it, and only
> God can maintain it...

It was a wonderful breakthrough, a move of God that many
of us would love to see in our lives and communities. We are
deceived if we think that such dealings of God are not
urgently needed in many of our churches today!

But there was more. Kuhn wrote:

> That night, after we had returned to our shanty, I said to
> my husband, 'John, that was more than your own
> inspiration. I'm going to note this date down and see –
> I'm sure someone in the homelands has been very
> specially praying for us.' And the date went down in
> my diary...

The Kuhns moved on elsewhere in their work. Some two
months passed. Then a letter came from a dear prayer-
warrior, Mrs K, who lived in a small town in North America.
It read something like this:

> I must write and tell you what happened today. All
> morning I could not do my housework, because of the
> burden on me concerning the Three Clan Village, so
> finally I went to the telephone and called Mrs W. She
> said that she had been feeling the very same way and
> suggested that we phone Mrs J and all go to prayer. We
> did so, each in her own kitchen, this morning we spent
> in intercession for those quarrelling clans. We feel God
> has answered. You will know.

After reading the letter, Isobel consulted her dairy. She
comments:

> Night with us is morning with them. It was the very time
> that we felt the 'astounding change' of which I had
> written in the circular. It was the same twenty-four hours
> that the clan arrows were burned! Now these prayer-
> warriors were not seemingly of the earth's mighty ones.
> Mrs K was delicate, had a heart condition. Mrs W was
> expecting a serious operation, and Mrs J was going blind.

All three were elderly women, too frail physically to cross the small town and gather in one place, but each in her own kitchen was joined to the others in spirit and the strength of that extra intercession, in addition to that which all the prayer-helpers were sending forth, pushed the battle over the wall ... for the liberating of a human soul, or a village of souls. ... The unseen missionary, the prayer-helper, has here an effectual weapon ... which is the last word in spiritual warfare. ... The missionary on the foreign field must likewise have other spirits to aid him with the battle in the heavenlies. Explain it as you wish, it is a fact, **and it works**. ... By March the friends at home had received our appeal for prayer, and had gone to their knees in intercession. Then, and then only, this little corner of Satan's kingdom began to shake. We felt it. ... The last two days ... **without any explanation that we could discover** a sudden and astounding change took place.

What will it take? *That* is what it will take in our generation. It will take the same partnership as there was then between those on the field and those in the sending churches at home, both playing their part, both taking their place in support of the national Churches they serve.

- John and Isobel Kuhn in their generation, along with many others, went to a foreign and unfamiliar land. They left homes and careers, comfort and familiarity, embracing new peoples and cultures, and thus saw the gospel change a multitude of lives. They were willing to **go**.

- Churches gave sacrificially in financial terms, so that the Kuhns and others could go to the field. They diverted money from their local church projects and gave to the work of world missions. They were willing to **give**.

- Mrs W, Mrs J and Mrs K prayed. They too surrendered themselves to be living sacrifices, and God came on the frail altar and lit their sacrifices with Holy Spirit anointing. They were available to **pray**.

And the result was rejoicing in heaven for the many Lisu there who came into the kingdom, including dear Mr Luda-Lamb! It took each one in the churches, at home and on the field, to take their place for battle. It will take no less today.

One final world from Isobel Kuhn. She finished that section of the book with a powerful comment, no less compelling and demanding today than when she wrote it fifty years ago:

> **The Lisu work has had wonderful prayer-warriors in the past; but many of them have been translated into His Presence. We are needing prayer-warrior reinforcements. And China, all China, needs them too.**   (emphasis mine)

Now, once more, the generation to which she wrote has mostly been translated into His Presence – including the saints from Three Clans, the Kuhns and the three old ladies who prayed so faithfully. A new generation must take their place, involving themselves with the same commitment at home and in the nations with God's ends of the earth agenda. Churches must embrace that divine imperative (Acts 13:1–3).

Our world is changing vastly in previously unimagined ways. But this challenge of the nations does not. No new technology, no modern sophistication can dispense with the call of God – for pray-ers, for givers and for goers. You and I in our day have to hear the Lord, and make our decision before Him. If we do not, fifty years on, 'Three Clans Village' in our new world will remain in darkness, and Mr Luda-Lamb will pass into a Christless eternity, the victim perhaps of some unresolved village feud.

What will it take to finish this task of reaching China with the gospel, of serving its growing Church? It will take men and women, in our new day, who will hear the voice of the Lord – and obey.

> *I heard the voice of the Lord, saying: 'Whom shall I send, and who will go for Us?' Then I said, 'Here am I! Send me.' And He said, 'Go, and tell this people . . . '*   (Isaiah 6:8–9)

Note

1.   All quotations in this chapter are taken from *Nests above the Abyss* by Isobel Kuhn (CIM/OMF), pp. 197–201. The relevant chapter title, significantly, is 'The Unseen Missionaries'.

Appendices

Appendix 1

The Minority Peoples of China

The Minority Nationalities of China (1990)

Name	Population	Language family	Location
Achang	27,708	Tibeto-Burman	Yunnan
Bai	1,594,827		Yunnan
Benglong	12,295 (1982)	Mon-Khmer	Yunnan
Bulang	82,280	Mon-Khmer	Yunnan
Bonan	12,212	Mongolian	Gansu
Bouyei	2,545,092	Tai	Guizhou
Dai	1,025,128	Tai	Yunnan
Daur	121,357	Mongolian	Manchuria
Deang	15,462		Yunnan
Dong	2,514,014	Tai	Guizhou
Dongxiang	373,872	Mongolian	Gansu
Drung	5,816	Tibeto-Burman	Yunnan
Evenki	26,315	Tungus	Manchuria
Gao Shan	2,909 (China)	Austronesian	Taiwan
Gelao	437,997		Guizhou
Han (Chinese)	1,042,482,187	Sinitic	Everywhere
Hani	1,253,952	Tibeto-Burman	Yunnan
Hezhen	4,245	Tungus	Manchuria
Hui	8,806,978	Sinitic	Everywhere
Jing	18,915		Guangxi
Jingpo	119,209	Tibeto-Burman	Yunnan
Jinuo	18,021	Tibeto-Burman	Yunnan
Kazakh	1,111,718	Turkic	Xinjiang
Kirghiz	141,549	Turkic	Xinjiang
Korean	1,902,597	Manchurian	
Lahu	411,476	Tibeto-Burman	Yunnan
Lhoba	2,312	Tibeto-Burman	Tibet
Li	1,110,900	Tai	Hainan Island

Name	Population	Language family	Location
Lisu	574,856	Tibeto-Burman	Yunnan
Manchu	9,821,180	Tungus	North
Maonan	71,968	Tai	Guangxi
Miao	7,398,035	Miao-Yao	South
Moinba	7,475	Tibeto-Burman	Tibet
Mongolian	4,806,849	Mongolian	North
Monguor (Tu)	191,624	Mongolian	Qinghai
Mulam	159,328	Tai	Guangxi
Naxi	278,009	Tibeto-Burman	Yunnan
Nu	27,123	Tibeto-Burman	Yunnan
Oroqen	6,965	Tungus	Manchuria
Pumi	29,657	Tibeto-Burman	Yunnan
Qiang	198,252	Tibeto-Burman	Sichuan
Russian	13,504	Indo-European	Xinjiang
Salar	87,697	Turkic	Qinghai
She	630,378	Miao-Yao	Fujian
Shui	345,993	Tai	Guizhou
Tajik	33,538	Indo-European	Xinjiang
Tatar	4,873	Turkic	Xinjiang
Tibetan	4,593,330	Tibeto-Burman	Tibet
Tujia	5,704,223		Hunan
Uighur	7,214,431	Turkic	Xinjiang
Uzbek	14,502	Turkic	Xinjiang
Wa	351,974	Mon-Khmer	Yunnan
Xibo	172,847	Tungus	North
Yao	2,134,013	Miao-Yao	South
Yugur	12,297	Turkic	Gansu
Yi	6,572,173	Tibeto-Burman	South
Zhuang	15,489,630	Tai	Guangxi
Unidentified	749,341		

References

Covell, Ralph R., *The Liberating Gospel in China: The Christian Faith Among China's Minority Peoples* (USA: Baker House, 1995).

Lewis, Jonathan (ed.), *The Condensed World Mission Book* (Philippines: Church Strengthening Ministry, 1996).

Stearns, Bill and Amy, *Catch the Vision 2,000* (USA: Bethany House Publishers, 1991).

Winter, Ralph D. and Hawthorne, Steven C. (eds), *Perspectives On the World Christian Movement – A Reader*, revised edition (USA: William Carey Library, 1999).

Appendix 2

Book Titles Available in Chinese

The following books in Chinese are available at CCSM or DPM addresses (see Appendix 4) to assist in outreach to Mainland Chinese students or workers. Most titles are translated so can also be obtained in English.

Books on the foundations of the Christian faith

CCS–1	*Covenant and the Kingdom* (CSM)
CCS–6	*Foundations of Christian Doctrine* (Kevin Connor)
CCS–7	*Abundant Life* (SEAN)
CCS–8	*First Steps*
CCS–10	*Following Jesus*
CCS–11	*Living God's Way* (Arthur Wallis)
CCS–14	*Starting from Zero*
CCS–15	*Abundant Light* (SEAN)
CCS–16	*Foundations of Christian Living* (Bob Gordon)
DPM–1	*Foundation Series* (Derek Prince)
DPM–2	*Self Study Bible Course* (Derek Prince)

Books on specific subjects

CCS9–1/3/7	*Christian Faith/Repentance/Righteousness*
CCS9–21/16/15	*Faith/Trust/Honour and Respect*
CCS9–10/28	*Evangelism/Mission*
CCS–12	*New Covenant Realities*

CCS–13	*Six in One* (6 smaller books in one on assurance of salvation, the church, etc.)
DPM–3	*Faith to Live By* (Derek Prince)
DPM–5/6/14	*Fatherhood/How to pass from curse to blessing/If you want God's best* (Derek Prince)
DPM–8–11	*Praying (for the Government)/Spiritual Warfare/Baptism in the Holy Spirit/Holy Spirit in You* (Derek Prince)
DPM–13/19/7	*Extravagant Love/God's Medicine Bottle/ Fasting* (Derek Prince)
DPM–18/24	*Grace of Yielding/Take heed that you are not deceived* (Derek Prince)
DPM–16/23	*Does your tongue need healing?/God's remedy for rejection* (Derek Prince)
DPM–21	*The Marriage Covenant* (Derek Prince)
DPM–26	*Blessing or Curse: You Can Choose* (Derek Prince)

Appendix 3

Recommended Reading

Adeney, David H., *China: The Church's Long March* (USA: Regal Books, and Overseas Missionary Fellowship, 1985)

Broomhall, A., *J. Hudson Taylor and China's Open Century*, 7 vols (Hodder and Stoughton Ltd and Overseas Missionary Fellowship)

Brother David, *God's Smuggler to China* (Hodder and Stoughton Ltd, 1981)

Crossman, Eileen Fraser, *Mountain Rain* (Overseas Missionary Fellowship, 1982)

Danyun, *Lilies Amongst Thorns* (Sovereign World, 1992)

Francis, Lesley, *Winds of Change* (Overseas Missionary Fellowship, 1985)

Kauffman, P.E., *China the Emerging Challenge: A Christian Perspective* (Grand Rapids, USA: Baker, 1981)

Kuhn, Isobel, *Nests above the Abyss* (Overseas Missionary Fellowship, 1947)

Lambert, Tony, *Resurrection of the Chinese Church* (Hodder and Stoughton Ltd and Overseas Missionary Fellowship, 1991)

Lawrence, Carl, *The Church in China: How it Survives and Prospers Under Communism* (Minneapolis, USA: Bethany House, 1985)

Lyall, L.T., *God Reigns in China* (Hodder and Stoughton Ltd, 1985); *New Spring in China* (Grand Rapids, USA: Zondervan, 1985)

MacInnis, Donald E., *Religious Policy and Practice in Communist China* (Hodder and Stoughton Ltd, 1972)

Monsen, Marie, *The Awakening: Revival in China 1927–1937* (Overseas Missionary Fellowship, English version 1961)

Morrison, Peter, *Making Friends with Mainland Chinese Students* (ISCS and OMF, 1995)

Paterson, Ross and Farrell, Elisabeth, *China: The Hidden Miracle* (Sovereign World, 1993)

Paterson, Ross, *Explaining Mission* (Sovereign World, 1994)

Pirolo, Neal, *Serving as Senders* (OM Publications)

Wallis, Arthur, *China Miracle* (Kingsway Publications, 1985)

Wang Mingdao, *A Stone Made Smooth* (Mayflower Books, 1981)

Secular titles, giving insight into recent Chinese history

Butterfield, Fox, *China: Alive in the Bitter Sea* (Hodder and Stoughton Ltd, 1983)

Chang, Jung, *Wild Swans* (HarperCollins, 1993)

Cheng, Nien, *Life and Death in Shanghai* (HarperCollins, 1993)

Appendix 4

Ministry Addresses

For further information on the situation in the Church in China and what you can do to help, please write to your local AM/CCSM office or the DPM-China office:

Antioch Missions, PO Box 2046, Robinson Road Post Office, Singapore 904046

Chinese Church Support Ministries, PO Box 2187, Warwick, WA 6024, Australia

Chinese Church Support Ministries, 2nd Floor, Silver Street Chambers, 12 Silver Street, Bury, Lancashire BL9 0EX, England

Chinese Church Support Ministries e.V., PO Box 180 164, 47171 Duisburg, Germany

Chinese Church Support Ministries, c/o Roland Kok, 41 Jalan Bakawali 54, Taman Johor Jaya, 81100 Johor Bahru, Malaysia

Chinese Church Support Ministries, PO Box 7156, Taradale, Napier, New Zealand

Chinese Church Support Ministries, PO Box 47, 75011 Uppsala, Sweden

Chinese Church Support Ministries, c/o 998 Kraanvoel Avenue, Silverton 0184, Pretoria, South Africa

Chinese Church Support Ministries, PO Box 26–58, Taichung, Taiwan R.O.C.

Chinese Church Support Ministries, c/o 232 Carey Avenue, Louisville, KY 40218, USA

DPM – China, PO Box 2046, Robinson Road Post Office, Singapore 904046

DPM International, PO Box 19824, Charlotte, North Carolina 28219–9824, USA

Or visit the ministry websites:

www.am-ccsm.org or www.derekprince.com

If you have enjoyed this book and would like to help us to send a copy of it and many other titles to needy pastors in the **Third World**, please write for further information or send your gift to:

Sovereign World Trust
PO Box 777, Tonbridge
Kent TN11 0ZS
United Kingdom

or to the **'Sovereign World'** distributor in your country.